"*Why Celibacy?* is not only the title of an important study by Fr. Carter Griffin, it is a question on the minds of many in today's society—including Catholics and even priests. Fr. Griffin addresses this question in a powerfully positive manner, stressing the important link between celibacy and paternity. Priesthood is defined not merely by what a priest does, but more importantly by who a priest is. The priest is a spiritual father and celibacy is an often under-appreciated element in the fruitfulness of his priestly ministry. I recommend this book to all who wish to understand and even reclaim celibacy as a precious gift entrusted to the Church by 'the Father, from whom every family in heaven and on earth is named' (Eph 3:15)."

MOST REV. PAUL S. COAKLEY
Archbishop of Oklahoma City

"A few years after I was ordained, my father died. In the midst of my sadness and sense of loss, I was struck by the realization of how much my father prepared me to be a priest by just being a good father. Fr. Griffin puts into words what I had intuited years ago—a celibate priest is not less of a father but more of a father to those entrusted to his spiritual care.

Fr. Carter Griffin offers more than an apologetic on celibacy. He launches a rescue mission to save the celibate priesthood from being reduced to something unnatural, anachronistic, and repressive. He shows just how celibacy is an efficacious sign of supernatural fecundity and how living it well must be rooted in spiritual fatherhood.

It is true that celibacy is not essential to the Sacrament of Holy Orders. Nevertheless, it is eminently suitable to the priesthood, as Fr. Griffin eloquently writes. It enables a priest not only 'to live his own supernatural fatherhood with greater efficacy and naturalness' but it also reveals the 'Fatherhood of God in a particularly striking way.'

We need a book like this. Many difficulties in the Church today could have been avoided if priests and bishops had lived celibacy well and truly been fathers. As rector of a major seminary, I know well that the needed reform in the Church today unavoidably begins with good priestly formation—and good priestly formation includes a robust formation in living celibacy well. Fr. Griffin clearly shows that we need celibacy now more than ever—and a celibate priesthood of true, spiritual fathers."

REV. MSGR. ANDREW R. BAKER, S.T.D.
Rector, Mount St. Mary's Seminary, Emmitsburg, MD

"The Church teaches that every man is called to be a father and every woman is called to be a mother. Fr. Carter Griffin has given us a brilliant and lucid presentation of the purposes and benefits of celibacy and the profundity of priestly paternity. This book is so needed in the Church at this time. Seminarians who read this will be excited about the gift of celibacy, and priests will be renewed in their commitment!"

FR. BRETT BRANNEN
Author and Pastor, Church of the Most Blessed Sacrament, Savannah, GA

"What an encouragement for priests in these challenging times! Fr. Griffin's careful study is an antidote to the impoverished understanding of the priesthood that is prevalent today. His careful reading of Scripture illuminates the profound relationship between priestly celibacy and spiritual fatherhood. *Why Celibacy?* is essential reading for priests and those who form them."

DR. MARY HEALY
Sacred Heart Major Seminary, Detroit, MI

"A thoughtful, trenchant, inspiring, and very timely defense of the ancient tradition of celibacy in the Latin-rite Catholic priesthood, written by one of America's finest priests."

GEORGE WEIGEL
Distinguished Senior Fellow and William E. Simon Chair in Catholic Studies Ethics and Public Policy Center

"This book has the timing of a divine intervention. Just when fatherhood, natural and priestly, appears to be in tatters, this book arrives with healing and bracing truth! Within the spousal gift that is priestly celibacy—a gift which is nothing less than a man's own body offered in response to God's love and the urgent spiritual needs of the Church—lies not simply sacrifice but generativity. It is the truth of spiritual generativity that has lay fallow in the consciousness of priests for too long. Now, what is implicit has become explicit with this clearly written and delightfully succinct book. Not only should every seminary require this as reading, every parish priest should read it together with the dads of his parish.

Through such efforts by seminaries and parish priests will come a renewal of reverence for fatherhood in our Church that will, hopefully, even affect Western culture."

DCN. JAMES KEATING
Institute for Priestly Formation, Creighton University, Omaha, NE

"Fr. Carter Griffin has done a great service for the Church by restoring to the discussion of priestly celibacy the often-forgotten dimension of spiritual fatherhood. This book is a must-read for seminarians, priests, and anyone desiring to understand the beautiful charism of celibacy."

FR. PAUL SCALIA
Episcopal Vicar for Clergy, Diocese of Arlington

"I highly recommend *Why Celibacy?* It is a very timely and provocative book that addresses the current crisis of fatherhood, the priesthood, and clerical celibacy with a clear and theologically well-grounded argument. It makes the case that priests do not renounce fatherhood but embrace celibacy as a privileged way of living it: generating life and fulfilling the fatherly responsibilities of providing for, guiding and teaching, and protecting those entrusted to their care. This compelling vision of the priest is rooted in his identity as sacramentally conformed to Christ the Head of the Church who perfectly represents and reveals God the Father."

SR. SARA BUTLER, M.S.B.T.
University of St. Mary of the Lake, Mundelein, IL

"One of the largest crises facing the Church comes from priests who do not love God's children as true spiritual dads, flowing from a defective understanding and living of priestly celibate chastity. To that malady Fr. Griffin provides a cure in this clear, concise and compelling presentation of how priestly celibacy enhances priestly fatherhood. This work will nourish priests and future priests for generations to come, strengthen every Catholic's appreciation for the treasures of the priesthood and priestly celibacy, and help men young and old grasp and grow in the capacity for chastity and authentic fatherhood. The reform of the Church will not happen without the reform of the priesthood Fr. Griffin engagingly describes in the precious book you now hold in your hands."

FR. ROGER J. LANDRY
Author of Plan of Life: Habits to Help You Grow Closer to God

WHY CELIBACY?

WHY CELIBACY?

RECLAIMING THE FATHERHOOD OF THE PRIEST

FR. CARTER GRIFFIN
Foreword by Scott Hahn

EMMAUS ROAD
PUBLISHING

Steubenville, Ohio
www.emmausroad.org

Emmaus Road Publishing
1468 Parkview Circle
Steubenville, Ohio 43952

Library of Congress Control Number: 2019939351
ISBN 978-1-949013-31-3

Cover image: Ordenación y primera misa de san Juan de Mata (ca. 1634) by Vincente Carducho, Museo del Prado, Madrid, Spain
Cover design and layout by Emily Feldkamp

Nihil Obstat:
The Reverend James Dunfee
Censor Librorum

Imprimatur:
The Most Reverend Jeffrey M. Montforton
Bishop of Steubenville
February 9, 2019

The nihil obstat and imprimatur are official declarations that a book or pamphlet is free of doctrinal or moral error. No implication is contained therein that those who have granted the nihil obstat and imprimatur agree with the contents, opinions or statements expressed.

Dedication

To the seminarians whom I have had the privilege to serve. Their courage, generosity, and nobility of heart in these troubled times have been an unwavering inspiration to me. This book, however inadequately, is a grateful and heartfelt tribute to them.

Table of Contents

Foreword

"STAY WITH ME," said Micah, "and be to me a father and a priest" (Judg 17:10).

"Come with us," urged the Danites, "and be to us a father and a priest" (Judg 18:19).

This fact—the fatherhood of priesthood—is at the heart of biblical religion, and is evident in the heartfelt pleas of Micah and the Danites.

The life of Israel required the service of a sacrificing priest. And the need did not go away with the arrival of the Messiah. Biblical religion is sacrificial, and sacrifice is a priestly act. Christ is our high priest, but he shares his ministry with those who are ordained to offer sacrifice in the Church.

Priesthood, however, is not simply a job, or a career path, or a sideline. It's a life, a vocation, a family bond. That is evident in the inspired words from the Book of Judges: "Stay with me . . . Come with us . . . Be a father to us." A priest is a father, and a father stays with his family and goes where they go. His commitment is total. He cannot conceive of a life apart from them.

Throughout the history of salvation, celibacy has safeguarded that commitment. In the Old Covenant, Israel's priests observed sexual continence during their rotating terms of service (see Exod 19:15 and Deut 23:9–13). At the conclusion of their term, they returned to their wives; but during their term they belonged entirely to God and the service of his chosen people.

In the New Covenant we see the fulfillment of priesthood in Jesus Christ. He is the "high priest of the good things that have come" (Heb 9:11). He is the model and image of what a priest should be. And he is celibate. His term of service is forever. It is perpetual, as his priesthood is eternal.

This book by Fr. Carter Griffin brings another feature of Jesus' priesthood into sharp focus. *Why Celibacy?* proposes that Scripture and the Church Fathers reveal all of our Lord's actions—his preaching and teaching, his relationships, his sacrifice on Calvary—as hallmarks of a faithful priest *and* actions of a faithful father.

Fatherhood is essential to the ministerial priesthood. A priest presides over the Mass. He is often the administrator of a parish. But, first and foremost, he is a spiritual father.

Jesus, who ordained the Apostles to share his ministry, told them that there would be a place for celibacy in the Church (Matt 19:10–12). St. Paul embraced that vocation (see 1 Cor 7) and relished the freedom it gave him for ministry. He was completely available to his congregations. He recognized, moreover, that he owed his freedom to his celibacy (see 1 Cor 7:32–34). His heart was undivided, his mind undistracted. He did not need to hesitate before placing himself in harm's way. He did not need to worry about appearing to show favoritism to a wife or children. He could be to the Church—wholeheartedly—"a father and a priest."

The Church of Jesus Christ has always followed the model of Jesus and Saint Paul. I do not mean to say that celibacy is always and everywhere mandatory. That is not the case. It is always, however, observed in some measure. In the Eastern Churches a married man may be ordained to priesthood, but the episcopate is reserved to celibates. A man, moreover, may not marry after ordination and remain active in priestly ministry. In the East it is customary also for married priests to observe periodic continence, as the Levites did in Israel.

In the West, it seems, the tradition of celibate priesthood is ancient indeed. A bishop of the fourth century, Saint Ambrose of Milan, assumes when he addressed his young clergy that many of them had never even heard of a married priest.

Celibate priesthood is a constant in biblical religion, and it is perfectly fulfilled in Christ and his body, the Church.

Fr. Griffin points out that throughout the Church's long history, wherever celibacy is lived well by priests, spiritual paternity follows. In this light, the seeming contradiction of the celibate father is no contradiction.

As Jesus knew, and as St. Paul knew, and as every Catholic priest knows, celibate priesthood has its practical advantages. I can testify to these as a counter-witness because I served as a married Presbyterian minister, and I struggled to balance my commitments. I saw that many of my colleagues were failing in their struggle—either favoring family over congregation or vice versa, and sometimes falling into adultery and divorce.

This is not to say that celibates never fail in their own struggles. They do, as the news media are eager to remind us. But marriage would, I think, exacerbate rather than solve their problems.

What we want from our clergy is what Micah wanted

and what the Danites wanted. We want them to be priests who not only offer sacrifice, but offer themselves entirely in sacrifice for their Church—just as fathers offer themselves in sacrifice for their families. We want them to be with us and to be Christ among us. We want them to stay with us as he stays with us.

This is a desire deep in our hearts because God placed it there.

Celibate priesthood is more than a custom for us. It is integral to tradition, from the Old Covenant through the New and into the age of the Church.

Why Celibacy? gets to the heart of this reality and offers the Church and her priests a renewed vision of the priesthood. More than that, Fr. Griffin offers a path forward for all men to become spiritual fathers in the order of grace. We should expect nothing less from Christ's priests.

Scott Hahn

Preface

ON APRIL 8, 2005, the largest congregation of Christian faithful in history gathered in St. Peter's Square for the funeral of Pope John Paul II. Kings and Presidents, religious and lay faithful, Catholics and non-Catholics, from every corner of the globe, came to pray and to show their love for a man who had touched countless souls over the course of his long life. With over four million mourners in attendance and billions of viewers on television, the recurring image evoked was that of a father's burial. When his simple casket was lowered in a final salute before the pallbearers bore it into the Basilica, few were able to restrain their tears as they bade farewell to their "Papa"—their "Father"—who had loved them with a father's heart generously, heroically, to his final breath.

In what many would see as a contradiction in terms, the man who modeled paternity for a generation of believers was a celibate priest. But a deeper understanding of priestly celibacy and spiritual fatherhood shows that it is no contradiction at all.

There is, I believe, a particular need for this deeper understanding. The scandal of unfaithful celibate priests and the legitimate sense of betrayal on the part of the faithful, as well as the shortage of priests, has seriously weakened confidence in the wisdom of priestly celibacy. As understandable as that reaction might be, I believe misgivings of celibacy are misplaced. Just as marriage does not cause adultery, the sexual abuse of minors and vulnerable adults is not caused by celibacy. When priests or bishops become dangerous predators and superiors do not stop them, it is not a failure of celibacy—it is a failure to live celibacy *well*. It is a failure of chastity, not celibacy. It is, in fact, a failure to live celibacy as priestly fathers. Good fathers simply do not abuse their children, and they tolerate no one who might.

Far from justifying an abolition or abridgement of celibacy, the storm of scandals in the Church today demands a profound renewal of celibate priesthood and the fatherhood to which it is ordered. I pray that this book may contribute in some small way to that renewal.

The aim of this book, however, goes beyond a response to these staggering betrayals of trust. I hope that it might also help to renew confidence in the powerful efficacy of priestly celibacy. As recently as 2013 the Church affirmed that celibacy "is a joyful gift which the Church has received and wishes to retain, convinced that it is a good for itself and for the world."[1] In 1992 St. John Paul II stated that the Synod of Bishops did "not wish to leave any doubts in the mind of anyone regarding the Church's firm will to maintain the law that demands perpetual and freely chosen celibacy for present and future candidates for priestly ordination in the Latin rite. The synod would like to see celibacy presented and explained . . . as a precious gift given

---

[1] Congregation for the Clergy, *Directory for the Life and Ministry of Priests* (Citta del Vaticano: Libreria Editrice Vaticana, 2013), no. 79.

by God to his Church and as a sign of the kingdom which is not of this world."[2]

Nevertheless, many priests, even some younger men formed after the seminary reforms of St. John Paul II, struggle mightily to live celibacy faithfully and too many are still leaving active ministry. In exploring the foundations of priestly celibacy, then, it is my aim not only to reinforce the ancient wisdom of the Church but also to remind priests why they have embraced it. St. Teresa of Calcutta once remarked that "priestly celibacy is that gift which prepares for *life in heaven*. Jesus calls his priest to be his co-worker in the Church, to fill heaven with God's children."[3] When Mother Teresa's insight about the fruitfulness of celibacy becomes an unshakeable conviction in the heart of a priest, he begins to see his celibacy, his priesthood, and his very life differently: he sees them in the light of paternity. He begins to see himself as a father in the order of grace, not only in name and in title but as an identity that permeates his entire priestly life. This book is therefore intended to confirm priests in the wisdom, beauty, and fruitfulness of their celibate priesthood.

Curiously, the spiritual fatherhood of celibate priests has received little attention in theology, perhaps in part because it has simply been taken for granted. Especially in

---

[2]   Pope John Paul II, Post-Synodal Apostolic Exhortation on the Formation of Priest in the Circumstances of the Present Day *Pastores Dabo Vobis* (March 15, 1992), § 29.

[3]   Teresa of Calcutta, "Priestly Celibacy: A Sign of the Charity of Christ" (1993): accessed October 5, 2018, http://www.vatican.va/roman_curia/congregations/cclergy/documents/rc_con_cclergy_doc_01011993_sign_en.html., emphasis in original.

regions where they commonly are called "Father," priests may implicitly acknowledge their own paternity without, perhaps, a clear grasp of its nature or how it is exercised. Some might allow, for instance, that in the administration of Baptism, priests enjoy a kind of spiritual paternity, but would struggle to distinguish it from that of laypeople or even nonbelievers administering the sacrament.

Beyond Baptism, the priest's paternity is seldom connected to his celebration of the other sacraments or with his preaching, teaching, shepherding, or temporal administration and governance. Still less is the priest's fatherhood associated with his commitment to celibacy. Indeed, celibacy is usually identified with the very renunciation of fatherhood. In short, while there may be an unformed idea that celibate priesthood has something to do with paternity, the actual application often seems obscure.

In response to this theological gap, St. Paul VI, in his encyclical *Sacerdotalis Caelibatus*, invited believers and theologians to study celibacy in the light of Christ's redemptive mission, "to persevere in the study of this vision, and to go deeply into the inner recesses and wealth of its reality. In this way, the bond between the priesthood and celibacy will more and more be seen as closely knit—as the mark of a heroic soul and the imperative call to unique and total love for Christ and His Church."[4] At a time when priestly celibacy is often seen as an arbitrary and anachronistic imposition, it is more important than ever to take up Pope Paul's challenge to discover the natural and supernatural logic inscribed in celibacy.

---

[4] Pope Paul VI, Encyclical Letter on the Celibacy of the Priest *Sacerdotalis Caelibatus* (June 24, 1967), § 25.

The conviction expressed in these pages is that priests embrace celibacy as a radical choice to give themselves to God and neighbor in such a way that they are enabled to generate new spiritual life. Priests are celibate, in short, because their celibacy—when lived well—is a privileged way of embracing a fatherhood that transcends nature alone; it is "supernatural" fatherhood in the order of grace.[5]

The pastoral implications of this idea are not only for priests but for all the faithful. While the principal audience of this book consists of diocesan priests, seminarians, and those who select and form them, most of what follows is equally applicable to priests of religious congregations. A great deal is also relevant to those who embrace apostolic celibacy as laymen. Married people, too, benefit from a greater awareness of celibate priestly fatherhood. Just as families with a father tend to enjoy more unity and a clear sense of identity, so too do parishes and dioceses tend to thrive more with a priest or bishop who perceives his vocation as inherently paternal and who exercises a generous and self-sacrificing love. When the faithful value that kind of love and expect it from their pastors, they can do much to restore a firm sense of paternity in the priesthood. Men are wonderfully made to rise to expectations, and few can elicit a more generous response from the heart of a man than the

[5] Throughout this book I will use the terms "supernatural fatherhood" and the more common "spiritual fatherhood" interchangeably. In my opinion, though, the former term is more precise, since it avoids any semblance of anthropological dualism. Also, for some, "spiritual" might imply a degree of unreality or abstraction, as if spiritual fathers were simply like or comparable to "real" fathers. What I intend by supernatural paternity is not simply a similitude of fatherhood, but a manifestation of fatherhood itself, as will be explained in the chapters that follow.

expectation that he become a worthy father.

Celibacy, Priesthood, and Fatherhood

An indirect motivation for this book is to offer rational underpinnings for the very notion of "celibate priestly fatherhood" against the headwinds of certain contemporary ideas. Each of these three terms—celibacy, priesthood, and fatherhood—is today subject to an intellectual reduction or impoverishment.

Celibacy is often viewed as a merely negative choice, a renunciation alone, rendering virtually incomprehensible the notion of positive generativity among those who embrace it. This limited view of celibacy, though it is making a strong resurgence, did not originate with modernity. In ancient times, for instance, the reduction of celibacy tended to focus rather narrowly on achieving bodily purity and often was fueled by a dim view of corporality and human sexuality. Today the tendency is to reduce celibacy to a pragmatic calculation of time and availability for ministry. Priests themselves, some of whom may be struggling with celibacy and unacquainted with its deeper reasons, can be heard expressing this view. Even the far richer notion of celibate spousality, that of being "married to the Church," does not provide adequate emotional traction for many priests to see their way through the challenges of celibacy. The ordering to spiritual fatherhood, in contrast, can be a far more compelling vision of celibacy for many priests.

In addition to an impoverished view of celibacy, there is today a diminished concept of priesthood that focuses more on its functional, even bureaucratic, aspects than on its relational, personal, and paternal dimensions. The technical specialization of professional work since the Enlightenment has not spared the priesthood, which is increasingly regarded in a largely administrative light, as a series of ministerial tasks for which men are more or less technically competent and by which their efficiency is judged. The pace of life made possible by advances in technology and communication, the greater expectations placed on fewer priests, and the general growth in administrative duties all contribute to a feeling among many busy parish priests that not enough time is left for genuine pastoral ministry. Despite their best intentions and efforts, priests often lament that they do too little of the very things they looked forward to on the day of their ordination, the things that are the heart of their ministry: preaching, administering the sacraments, and spending time with their people. It is what a priest *does* rather than who a priest *is* that sometimes defines the vocation today in the mind of both the priest and his people. The view of the priestly life centered on programs, institutional ministries, and measurable success is a woefully depleted vision of the priesthood that can be remedied by a return to priestly paternity, as I hope to show.

The third intellectual reduction relevant to this discussion is an impoverished view of fatherhood itself. Today, many perceive fatherhood merely as a raw biological act—and even that biological contribution is being gradually eroded by medical advances. Beginning with the sexual revolution of the 1960's, but accompanied by more recent scientific advances in the areas of contraception, in vitro fertilization, surrogacy, and—soon enough—cloning, human sexuality has been gradually de-coupled from its natural ordering to human generation. While motherhood has also suffered from this depleted anthropology, the more detached physical and emotional part played by the man in human generation more easily obscures his contribution. As a result, Western society increasingly judges the man's familial role as dispensable. The damage caused to children, to mothers, to society at large, and to fathers themselves by this diminution of fatherhood is colossal. As research consistently shows, children who grow up without their fathers are dramatically more likely to fail at school, to experience emotional and behavioral problems, to abuse drugs, to suffer child abuse, and to wind up in prison.[6] Psychologist Paul Vitz notes that prisons in the United States, statistically speaking, are essentially facilities to house fatherless young men.[7] There is a desperate need to renew and restore our cultural reverence for the nobility of fatherhood.

These downward trends in our cultural understanding of celibacy, priesthood, and paternity are admittedly not universal, though I believe they are more deeply embedded than many wish to believe. Wherever they are found, a richer understanding of the spiritual fatherhood of celibate priests can help restore their luster. Recognizing the anemic and negative view of celibacy for what it is, we can begin to understand that the celibate commitment is positive and

---

[6] See for instance Wade F. Horn, "The Rise of an American Fatherhood Movement," in *The Faith Factor in Fatherhood: Renewing the Sacred Vocation of Fathering*, ed. Don E. Eberly (Lanham, MD: Lexington Books, 1999), 136. Also, Philip M. Sutton, "The Fatherhood Moment: The Rest of the Story," in *Marriage and the Common Good: Proceedings from the Twenty-Second Annual Convention of the Fellowship of Catholic Scholars, September 24–26, 1999, Deerfield, Illinois*, ed. Kenneth D. Whitehead (South Bend, IN: St. Augustine's Press, 2001), 62.

[7] See Paul C. Vitz, "The Importance of Fathers: Evidence from Social Science," 6, accessed October 11, 2018, https://www.catholiceducation.org/en/controversy/marriage/family-decline-the-findings-of-social-science.html.

generates life. Only then can the priesthood be freed from its burden of functionalism and reaffirmed as a vocation that embraces the whole man in a paternal identity directed to the generation of new children in grace. For true renewal within the Church to take place, fatherhood must be liberated from a materialistic, "biologistic" oversimplification and once again upheld as the highest fulfillment of masculinity, ordered both to the procreation of life and to its fruition— both naturally and supernaturally.[8]

Accentuating the spiritual paternity of celibate priests sheds new light on all three of these realities—celibacy, priesthood, and fatherhood—and helps to restore their full dignity and significance.

In fact, it is not only celibate priests who benefit from a better understanding of these important concepts but all Catholics. A former parishioner who is now a religious sister recently wrote to me about the impact of celibate priests in her life. I think she speaks for many of the faithful. "I'm not sure that I can put it into words very well," Sr. Diana Marie began. "I just know that priestly celibacy has impacted my life in a profound way. The difference that priests have made in my life, I am convinced, could not have been made

---

[8] The background of this book may be found in my doctoral dissertation entitled *Supernatural Fatherhood through Priestly Celibacy: Fulfillment in Masculinity (A Thomistic Study)* published in 2011 by the Pontifical University of the Holy Cross in Rome. In restructuring and condensing that work, and also adding new material, I have sought to make it more readable and less dense than an academic dissertation while still aiming at an audience that is familiar with the broad contours of the discussion of celibacy. Readers who wish for a more intensive academic study of the topic in general, including its relevance for the all-male priesthood and responding to its feminist critics, may wish to consult the dissertation.

by married men, married priests, or even faithful women. There is something unique and irreplaceable about the role a man entirely given over to God can play in a life." She then concluded, "My life is different because of priests who have given themselves over body and soul to the Lord and to the Church—or at least constantly strive to."[9]

I believe that this experience of priestly celibacy is common, but so is the struggle to articulate why exactly it has been spiritually fruitful in her life. "I'm not sure that I can put it into words very well," she wrote. Many would agree. Answering the question "Why celibacy?" has a particular urgency today. I hope that this book, by showing that celibacy is a privileged way of living spiritual fatherhood, will give a convincing and positive answer.

---

[9] Sister Diana Marie Andrews, OP, of the Dominican Sisters of Hawthorne, in private correspondence with the author, December 20, 2018.

The Celibate Fatherhood of Christ

AT THE NATIONAL GALLERY OF LONDON there is a painting by Sebastiano del Piombo showing Jesus raising Lazarus from the dead. In this image, the Lord is reaching out his arm toward Lazarus, who is emerging from the tomb wrapped in linens, with his sisters Martha and Mary and the crowd looking on. Jesus' hand is in precisely the same posture as the hand of God the Father in Michelangelo's great fresco, the *Creation of Adam*, on the ceiling of the Sistine Chapel. Whether del Piombo intended it or not—the *Raising of Lazarus* was painted only six years after the Sistine Chapel—he made a very important and theologically profound statement about Jesus' action in raising his friend Lazarus from the dead. As God the Father gave life to the First Adam, so did Christ— the Last Adam—give new life to Lazarus and to the multitudes who came to him for mercy and truth and healing; and so too does this New Adam continue to give new life in grace to countless more through his perfect act of love on the Cross. Wittingly or not, del Piombo was harkening to an ancient undercurrent in Catholic thought that sees in Jesus not only the Son of the Father but a father himself of a new and redeemed humanity.

The point is an important one. If the celibate priest is truly a *father* in any strong sense of the word, then theologically it must follow that Christ, in whose priesthood every priest shares, must himself also be a father in the order of grace.

While it may seem a little jarring to call Jesus a father, there is solid support for the idea in the Scriptures and in the theological tradition. Adam himself is the father of humanity, the one commissioned by God to "be fruitful and multiply" (Gen 1:28). Jesus, according to St. Paul, is "the last Adam" (1 Cor 15:45), identifying him as the new father of humanity, a father in the order of grace, who has been commissioned by God to "be fruitful and multiply" a redeemed human race, to generate children for the kingdom of heaven. There are hints of this in the Gospels as well. Though using an idiom, Jesus often employed the affectionate term "children" when addressing his disciples: "Children, how hard it is for those who trust in riches to enter the kingdom of God!" (Mark 10:24); "Little children, yet a little while I am with you" (John 13:33); "Children, have you any fish?" (John 21:5); "Child, your sins are forgiven" (Mark 2:5).

Most explicitly, in his ministry Jesus performs every action of the good father: he provides his disciples with food, both for their bodies and their souls, he guides and teaches them, and he protects them from harm. Above all, he gives them, and all believers, new life—the highest life of all—in the Paschal Mystery and prepares the way for their resurrection, their physical birth into eternal life. "For as the Father raises the dead and gives them life," writes St. John, "so also the Son gives life to whom he will" (John 5:21). St. John also refers to Christ's supernatural generativity in his first epistle: "And now, little children, abide in him, so that when he appears we may have confidence and not shrink from him in shame at his coming. If you know that he is righteous, you may be sure that everyone who does right is born of him" (1 John 2:28–29).

Exegetes have even found paternal references to Christ in the Old Testament, such as an oft-cited passage from Isaiah stating that the messianic King would be "father of the world to come" (Isa 9:6, DRA)[1] and another Isaian passage quoted by the Letter to the Hebrews, "Behold, I and my children, whom the LORD hath given me" (Isa 8:18, DRA, quoted in Heb 2:13). In the Suffering Servant passages of Isaiah, we read that "when he makes himself an offering for sin, he shall see his offspring, he shall prolong his days; the will of the LORD shall prosper in his hand" (Isa 53:10).

Theological reflection on Christ as father, though always an intellectual sub-current, endured in the patristic age and beyond.[2] Explicit reference to the fatherhood of Christ can, for instance, be found in the writings of Sts. Justin Martyr, Irenaeus of Lyons, Clement, Athanasius, Philomeno of Mabbug, Ephraim, and Benedict, as well as Origen, Evagrius of

---

[1] Sometimes translated as "Everlasting Father" or "Father-Forever."

[2] See José Granados, "Priesthood: A Sacrament of the Father," *Communio: International Catholic Review* 36, no. 2 (Summer 2009): 197–200. For a more complete study see Fernando Benicio Felices Sánchez, *La Paternidad Espiritual del Sacerdote: Fundamentos Teológicos de la Fecundidad Apostólica Presbiteral* (San Juan, Puerto Rico: San Juan de Puerto Rico, 2006).

Pontus, and Melito of Sardis. More implicitly it is found in writers such as Sts. Ambrose, Augustine, and Leo the Great. In later centuries, two of its greatest exponents were the Spanish writers Fray Luis de León and St. John of Avila. In Spain there is a "Christ the Father Cemetery," and in the Eastern Churches it is not uncommon to hear prayers to "Father Christ."

That the paternity of Christ remained a theme even of late medieval popular piety is reflected, for example, in the fifteenth-century English Christmas carol *This Endris Night*, which places these words on the lips of Mary:

> My Son, my Brother, Father, dear,
> Why liest Thou thus in hay?
> My sweetest bird, thus 'tis required,
> Though Thou be King veray;
> But nevertheless I will not cease
> To sing, By by, lullay.

Allusions to Christ's fatherhood, then, enjoy a respected, if somewhat less celebrated, pedigree in the theological tradition.

Embodying the Father's Paternity

Christ's fatherhood is both a visible representation and an agent of God the Father's paternity. Through his Sacred Humanity, Christ represents the Fatherhood of God more perfectly than any other being. Thus he tells Philip at the Last Supper, "He who has seen me has seen the Father" (John 14:9). Reflecting on this response, St. Thomas Aquinas comments that two people can be so alike that one may say,

"If you saw one you saw the other." Yet in human likeness, however similar various people may be, they always remain distinct individuals. The likeness of the divine Father and his eternal Son, however, is in the same divine nature, to which the Incarnate Son is united by the hypostatic union. Therefore, Aquinas concludes, "when seeing the Son, the Father is better seen than when seeing mere human likenesses, no matter how much alike they are."[3]

The reflection of the Father can be perceived in Jesus' life. An outstanding feature of his ministry was his merciful love, surely a distinguishing mark of his representation of God the Father. We only need to reflect on his extensive healing ministry, his tireless compassion for sinners and the downtrodden, and his parables of mercy, above all the "Magna Carta" of mercy in the parable of the Prodigal Son. Jesuit theologian Jean Galot speculates that there is even a kind of quasi-sacramental character impressed on the soul of Jesus that enables him uniquely to make visible God the Father.[4]

Jesus' humanity is not only representative of God the Father. It is itself an instrument of redemption, generating life as both Head and Bridegroom of the Church. As Adam is the father of the human race in creation, so the New Adam is the father of the human race in re-creation, in redemption. Christ merited the grace of regeneration—spiritual rebirth—in the Paschal Mystery, the source of his fatherhood in the order of grace. As head of the Church, Christ becomes "father"—first to Mary, then to the apostles, then

---

[3] St. Thomas Aquinas, *Super Evangelium S. Ioannis Lectura* (Rome: Marietti, 1972), 14, lec. 3.

[4] Jean Galot, *Theology of the Priesthood*, trans. Roger Balducelli (San Francisco: Ignatius Press, 1984), 203–204.

to all disciples through the ages. He invites his apostles to a communion with him that reflects the union he has with the Father.

At the Last Supper, for instance, Jesus assumes the paternal role in the ritual meal and prays to the Father "that they may all be one; even as you, Father, are in me, and I in you" (John 17:21). In that communion he exemplifies the love, compassion, patience, and fruitfulness that he then enjoins on his apostles. Like any father, his paternity does not end with generating life itself but includes its nourishment, protection, teaching, and all the other goods supplied by a father.

It is understandable that Jesus, seeking to affirm and reveal the Fatherhood of God, would not emphasize his own derived paternity. He does, however, frequently describe his relationship to the Church as that of a Bridegroom in a way that suggests paternity.[5] In Mark's Gospel, for example, when Jesus is asked why his disciples do not fast, he responds, "Can the children of the marriage fast, as long as the bridegroom is with them?" (Mark 2:19, DRA).[6] The implication is that Jesus is the Bridegroom of the Church because he is first a father—the disciples are already "children of the marriage" at the time of the nuptials.

The spousal claim of Christ, in other words, contains within it an implicit claim to paternity as well. As the New

---

[5] See Matt 9:15; Matt 25:1–13; Mark 2:19–20; Luke 5:34–35; John 3:29.

[6] The King James Version is even more precise than the Douay-Rheims, rendering the Greek (νυμφῶνος, *nymphōnos*) as "children of the bridechamber," though newer English translations tend to render it "wedding guests," presumably in order to avoid confusion regarding the image of a bridegroom with children. It is regrettable, however, since there is an important truth conveyed in so explicitly identifying Jesus' disciples as the "children of the marriage [or bridechamber]."

Adam, he is betrothed to the New Eve, represented by Mary and fulfilled in his Bride the Church, born, as the Fathers often say, from his side on the Cross. Christ's sacrifice is fruitful—that is, paternal—because the salvific grace that he merited on the Cross is implanted in his spotless Bride, who raises up offspring in the order of grace.

The fatherhood of Christ, the celibate High Priest of the New Covenant, provides the basis and template for celibate fatherhood in the ministerial priest. It also anticipates the dramatic center of the priest's fatherhood in the Holy Eucharist. Christ's own fatherhood is derived from his life-giving sacrifice on Calvary, a self-emptying love that is mirrored in his choice for celibacy. So too the spiritual fatherhood of the celibate priest. His re-presentation in the Mass of Christ's sacrifice is the source from which his priestly paternity flows. The witness of undivided love—that of Jesus and of his priest—is also, as we shall see, among the most compelling arguments for the wisdom of priestly celibacy.

Chapter One

Priestly Fatherhood

CARDINAL HENRY EDWARD MANNING, a nineteenth-century English prelate, was convinced of the profound importance of the priest's fatherhood. The "title of father is the first, the chief, the highest, the most potent, the most persuasive, the most honourable of all the titles of a priest," Cardinal Manning wrote. "He may receive from the world and from its fountains of honour many names, from the schools of learning many degrees, from the ecclesiastical law many dignities; but none has so deep and so high a sense as father." Significantly he adds, "And none but the spiritual fatherhood will pass into eternity."[1]

Priestly fatherhood is itself no surprise to most Catholics today. In countries like the United States, we even address our priests as "Father." The challenge is understanding what that fatherhood means. Where does it come from? What are its duties? How is it exercised? As a scientist who

---

[1] Henry Edward Manning, *The Eternal Priesthood* (Baltimore: John Murphy and Co., 1883), 30.

studies rivers must first understand the source from which they flow, the source from which they draw their vitality, our investigation into the various streams of fatherhood must begin at the source of their vitality in the very Fatherhood of God.

God the Father, Origin of All Fatherhood

Jesus told his disciples, "And call no man your father on earth, for you have one Father, who is in heaven" (Matt 23:9). These words from Scripture are sometimes employed to denounce the unscriptural foundations of priestly fatherhood. However, they are its clearest witness. They reveal the profound truth that all human fatherhood—including that of the celibate priest—is grounded in God's own paternity of the eternal Son, the Father being the source of all paternity in heaven and on earth, as St. Paul teaches the Ephesians (see Eph 3:15, DRA).

Catholic trinitarian theology has insisted through the centuries that the Scriptural data of Jesus' filial relationship to his Father need to be taken at face value. The Son is neither subordinate nor identical to the Father but genuinely his coeternal, divine Son. "This is my beloved Son," the Father declared at both Jesus' baptism and Transfiguration (Matt 3:17, 17:5; Mark 9:7; Luke 3:22, 9:35). Jesus, for his part, spoke often about his Sonship while also affirming his own divinity by urging faith in himself, accepting the worship and homage of men, working miracles in his own name, and performing divine actions, such as forgiving sins (e.g. Matt 9:2, 15:25, 28:18; Mark 8:38; Luke 7:48; John 14:1, 20:28; among many others). At one point he stunned his listeners by declaring, in the distinctive language of divinity, "Truly,

truly, I say to you, before Abraham was, I am" (John 8:58). The wording was so unmistakable that they tried, then and there, to stone him for it.

Jesus, then, is truly Son and truly God. It is easy to forget how radical that statement is. He is generated by the Father in such a way that God's substance is not divided, as a thought is generated from the intellect without dividing the intellect.[2] The substantial unity of the Father and the Son is so complete that they are not simply of the same species but in fact of the same form. God the Father is not only truly a father, he is the *truest* father since the Son is eternal, instant, and perfect. Every other example of paternity, including the fatherhood of men, is in comparison but a faint echo of its divine source.

Created Fatherhood

From this primordial fatherhood of God, a cascading paternity enters the created world. Jesus tells the Pharisees that God is "not God of the dead, but of the living" (Luke 20:38; Mark 12:27). God delights in giving life; the natural world simply teems with it. The sheer variety of plants and animals attest to the fact. Joseph Ratzinger, future Pope Benedict XVI, described the wonderful superabundance of life

---

[2]   St. Thomas explains that the likeness of the Son is precisely why the Son is "generated" while the Spirit is "spirated," which is an act of will rather than intellect; see Réginald Garrigou-Lagrange, *The Trinity and God the Creator*, trans. Frederic C. Eckhoff (St. Louis, MO: B. Herder Book Co., 1952), 66. See also Thomas Aquinas, *Summa Theologiae*, trans. Fathers of the English Dominican Province (New York: Benziger Bros, 1948), I, q. 27, a. 5; Thomas Aquinas, *On the Truth of the Catholic Faith (Summa Contra Gentiles) Book IV: Salvation*, trans. Charles J. O'Neil (New York: Hanover House, 1955), IV, chap. 23, no. 12.

that is written in the book of nature. "Excess," he writes, "is God's trademark in his creation."[3] But there is one thing even greater than generating life. It is generating others who generate life. God is not only a generator but a generator of generators. He is not only a Father but a Father of fathers. And that begins the "cascade" of fatherhood into the created order, beginning with the greatest of creatures, the angels.

St. Paul spoke of created "paternity in *heaven* and earth" (Eph 3:15, DRA, emphasis added), so it is not a stretch to attribute a certain analogous paternity to angels through their intercessory prayer and protective love. Aquinas argues that anyone "who communicates an act of life can be called a father. Therefore, whoever stimulates another to some vital act, whether it be to good activity, to understanding, to willing or loving, can be given the name of father." Thus, he continues, in the "acts by which one angel illumines, perfects, and purifies another, it is evident that that angel is the father of the other—just as a teacher is the father of his disciples."[4]

Elsewhere, St. Thomas attributes to angels the role of cleansing, enlightening, and instructing, preparing men to receive grace through their illuminations and protecting men as their spiritual guardians, all of which are paternal functions.[5] The *Catechism of the Council of Trent* touchingly describes the appointment of guardian angels as an expression of God's paternal solicitude for man:

[3] Joseph Ratzinger, *Introduction to Christianity*, trans. J. R. Foster (San Francisco: Ignatius Press, 1990), 197.

[4] St. Thomas Aquinas, *Super Epistolam ad Ephesios Lectura* (Rome: Marietti, 1953), 3, lec. 4.

[5] See Aquinas, *Summa Theologiae* I-II, q. 112, a. 1, ad 3.

> Just as parents, whose children are about to travel a dangerous and infested road, appoint guardians and helpers for them, so also in the journey we are making toward our heavenly country our heavenly Father has placed over each of us an Angel under whose protection and vigilance we may be enabled to escape the snares secretly prepared by our enemy, repel the dreadful attacks he makes on us, and under his guiding hand keep the right road.[6]

Nevertheless, though angels carry out many functions of fatherhood, they do not generate other angels. In fact, since the human mode of generation is a closer approximation to God's Fatherhood—generating a Son of the same nature—Aquinas singles out paternity as one way in which human beings surpass angels, who otherwise by nature are superior to men.[7] Human beings, then, enjoy the highest manifestation of fatherhood among creatures, generating—in a manner approximating God himself—rational persons, children destined for eternal life. The human vocation to motherhood and fatherhood enjoys the distinction of imitating the very paternity of God. Even unaided by revelation, human reason is able to perceive something of the greatness and dignity of generating children. With the benefit of revelation, though, we know that God intervenes in fashioning a unique immortal human soul in every person, raising the grandeur of human paternity to otherwise unimaginable heights.

---

[6] *Catechism of the Council of Trent*, trans. John A. McHugh and Charles Callan (Fort Collins, CO: Roman Catholic Books, 2002), 502.

[7] See Aquinas, *Summa Theologiae* I, q. 93, a. 3.

The Scriptures emphasize the derivation of human fatherhood from divine Fatherhood. In the beginning of the Book of Genesis, God says, "Let us make man in our image, after our likeness" (Gen 1:26). Several chapters later, when Eve gives birth to their first child, the Scriptures take pains to compare Adam's paternity to that of God. "When Adam had lived a hundred and thirty years, he became the father of a son *in his own likeness, after his image*, and named him Seth" (Gen 5:3, emphasis added). It is clear at the very beginning of the Bible that man's fatherhood generates in a way that parallels the generativity of God. When God made Adam and Eve and inscribed into their being the call to be fruitful, then, he was inscribing a part of himself into humanity. Human generation is not simply a mechanism for procreation; it is sharing in the very life of God.

In the New Testament, Jesus' use of the word *Abba* (Mark 14:36), normally employed in an intimate, familial setting, and his repeated reference to his Father (156 times in the Gospel of St. John alone) stresses the similarity between his divine Father and human fathers. For example, in St. Luke's Gospel, Jesus makes a direct comparison between human fatherhood and divine Fatherhood when he asks, "What father among you, if his son asks for a fish, will instead of a fish give him a serpent; or if he asks for an egg, will give him a scorpion? If you then, who are evil, know how to give good gifts to your children, how much more will the heavenly Father give the Holy Spirit to those who ask him!" (Luke 11:11–13).

Perhaps the clearest expression of the link between human and divine paternity, however, has already been mentioned—Jesus' warning to his disciples to "call no man your father on earth, for you have one Father, who is in heaven" (Matt 23:9). Since this admonition obviously cannot deny the natural fatherhood of men—he himself honored human fathers and lived under obedience to St. Joseph—it can only point to the source of fatherhood in God, from which all human fatherhood is derived.

Biological and Natural Fatherhood

Human paternity is found most immediately and most clearly in biological fatherhood. In the communion of human persons in which a man and a woman generate a third, God enters into that union and creates something that did not exist before, something totally beyond their capacity to generate: an immortal, rational, human soul destined for eternal life.

Biological fatherhood is the basis and template for all human fatherhood, the paternity that is most completely possessed by the man himself and which extends beyond the physical act of generation to the nourishment, guidance, and protection of his offspring. The man who, after conceiving a child, abandons him, is nonetheless still a father—however negligent he might be. Nonetheless, man's fatherhood is not simply biological, not ordered simply to the child's bare existence, but to his human development; not just to his generation but to his natural perfection. In contrast to *biological* fatherhood, this can be called *natural* fatherhood. It is realized when a man provides for his child, guides and teaches his son or daughter, and protects his child from harm.

A natural father is expected to provide his children with their material needs, such as food, clothing, shelter, and medical care. Often it is this fundamental duty that gives meaning to a father's manual or professional work, which otherwise may provide little personal satisfaction. A father also provides for the members of his family by giving them a cultural identity, a place in the world, a coordinating principle of life. The custom of wives and children taking the man's last name reflects this paternal function. His role in providing a family's identity, it seems to me, is often underestimated, though its importance becomes clearer in its absence. Emotional fragility, fierce rebellion, psychological and sexual confusion, an obsession with ceaseless affirmation, and a lack of confidence found in children all frequently stem from the absence of a father providing the security and stability of a familial and personal identity, and often a cultural and religious identity as well.[8]

After the basic temporal needs of children are met, a key responsibility of natural fatherhood is guiding and teaching offspring in a distinctively active, systematic, masculine way.[9] He educates and forms them in virtue and has a special capacity to foster the authentic freedom of his children and their potential for sacrificial love. He does this first by entering the "dyad" of the mother–child relationship in

---

[8] See Paul C. Vitz, "The Importance of Fathers: Evidence from Social Science," accessed October 11, 2018, https://www.catholiceducation.org/en/controversy/marriage/family-decline-the-findings-of-social-science.html.

[9] It is beyond the scope of this book, but among the many contemporary studies of the male-female difference, see, for instance, Simon Baron-Cohen's *The Essential Difference: Men, Woman, and the Extreme Male Brain*; Michael Gurian's *Boys and Girls Learn Differently!*; Steven Rhoads' *Take Sex Differences Seriously*; Leonard Sax' *Why Gender Matters*; Lewis Wolpert's *Why Can't a Man Be More Like a Woman? The Evolution of Sex and Gender*. This difference, of course, is also germane to the conversation about the all-male priesthood. See Manfred Hauke, *Women in the Priesthood? A Systematic Analysis in the Light of the Order of Creation and Redemption*, trans. David Kipp (San Francisco: Ignatius Press, 1988), 94.

order to help the child differentiate and distance himself, in a healthy sense, from his mother. One author on fatherhood writes that where "this initiative is energetic and winsome, developmental psychology teaches us, an essential autonomy from the mother is fostered and children of both sexes are significantly helped in orienting themselves to the cultural universe outside the home with its laws and ethical norms."[10]

Since the father–child bond is the first "social" relationship not based on the "primary bond" of mother–child or the "pair bond" of male–female, in a certain sense it is the foundation for all other social relationships.[11] Many perceive a sense of entitlement and egotism that disproportionately affects young people today. It can be traced, in part, to the failure of fathers to prepare the hearts of their children for self-giving love. Good fathers want their children to be free, not forever dependent, and ultimately able themselves to become generative parents of their own children. By opening up a healthy space between child and mother at the right time and in appropriate ways, the father helps his son or daughter begin to establish unique, personal relationships with others. He sets the child on a path which blossoms in the capacity to give himself or herself to another in sacrificial love.

---

[10] John W. Miller, *Biblical Faith and Fathering: Why We Call God 'Father'* (New York: Paulist Press, 1989), 57. Also see William May, "The Mission of Fatherhood," *Josephinum Journal of Theology* 9, no. 1 (Winter–Spring 2002): 49; Walter J. Ong, *Fighting for Life: Contest, Sexuality, and Consciousness* (Ithaca, NY: Cornell University Press, 1981), 174–175; and Monica Migliorino Miller, "The Gender of the Holy Trinity," *New Oxford Review* 70, no. 5 (May 2003): 28.

[11] See John W. Miller, "The Idea of God as Father," in *The Faith Factor in Fatherhood: Renewing the Sacred Vocation of Fathering*, ed. Don E. Eberly (Lanham, MD: Lexington Books, 1999), 208.

In addition to providing for his children and guiding their development, a father protects them from physical, emotional, and psychological harm. In the case of disciplining his children for their own good and leading his family with a clear but gentle authority, this protection is internally directed. Together with his wife, though with a masculine emphasis, a father has the obligation to correct his children when necessary and to put appropriate limits on their behavior. Through this discipline the father protects his children from their own misguided decisions and cultivates them in virtue. He is tasked with exercising a firm but humble authority that leads, nurtures, and unites.

While children (especially those of a very young age) will respect their father's rightful authority out of some measure of fear, a more long-lasting foundation of respect grows out of seeing his strong character in action: his moral strength, his vision for the family, and his assumption of responsibility. Sadly, this contrasts with many models of fatherhood, regrettably common today, that are basically selfish and narcissistic.[12] When children perceive that the good father's authority is not self-serving, that he is attuned to their needs and interested in his family, never violent, vengeful, coercive, or self-important, they are taught that the authority and power of their father—which is real—is nevertheless humble. Through it he protects his family from internal disorder by love, patience, and compassion, together with an honest clarity and, when necessary, disciplinary

---

[12] See Vitz, "The Importance of Fathers: Evidence from Social Science," 16–17. Also, Paul C. Vitz, "The Father Almighty, Maker of Male and Female," *Touchstone* 14, no. 1 (January–February 2001): 36.

punishment. As we shall see, all these qualities of a natural father's protective mission are also present in the spiritual paternity of the priest.

The father's protective role is external when it is directed against outside threatening forces, whether physical threats to family or moral threats, such as harmful ideologies taught in school, corrosive cultural influences, and dangers from the internet. There is a certain assertiveness in human males to which every parent and educator can attest. One thinker conjectures that the male embryo's production of testosterone in order to offset the countervailing tendencies of maternal hormones establishes him in a posture of resistance from the earliest weeks and months of his existence.[13] From age two, and perhaps earlier, this sense of environmental differentiation and conflict is expressed socially by young boys, who more often disobey, start fights, resist education, and stutter (a sign of conflict). While females tend to internalize information and understand subjective data better, males tend to focus on the objective situation, categorizing, systematizing, and, when necessary, modifying the environment. As a result, men are better adapted to meeting resistance and women to adjusting to the demands of a given situation.[14]

This greater capacity for conflict in men can be of great service to families. "God has created us men to be the ones who do not give birth," Professor Anthony Esolen writes, "and who therefore are, as a brute biological fact, dispensable. Therein lies our glory and the claim we justly make upon our wives. A man is indispensable, so to speak, only

---

[13] See Ong, *Fighting for Life: Contest, Sexuality, and Consciousness*, 68.
[14] See Hauke, *Women in the Priesthood?*, 88–92.

insofar as he assumes the danger of leading in faith and love. Such a man knows that the breath in his lungs is of no consequence."[15] Whatever the cause, when this masculine orientation toward conflict is properly channeled, men are better equipped to overcome the environment and their own personal feelings—and their weaknesses—in order to defend their families.

These three features of natural fatherhood—providing, guiding, and protecting—are essential for the flourishing of children. In a broader sense, they are also a compelling response to the impoverished contemporary view of fatherhood sketched in the preface of this book. Far from superfluous, fathers are irreplaceable contributors to the task of biological and natural generation. Nevertheless, their most distinguished claim to greatness lies still ahead.

Even as biological paternity points beyond itself to its fulfillment in natural paternity, so too does natural paternity point beyond itself to imparting life in the order of grace. A human child, after all, is not born simply for this temporal life, not born only to enjoy the goods of this world, but also—and even more so—to enjoy the imperishable goods of heaven. Every person is born for eternal life. Fathers and mothers are normally credited with the natural lives of their children, but their greatest achievement is in fostering their children's supernatural lives through their prayer, sacrifice, teaching of the faith, setting an example of Christian discipleship, bringing them to the sacraments, forming them

---

[15] Anthony Esolen, "Over Our Dead Bodies: Men Who Are Willing to Lay Down Their Lives Are Truly Indispensable," *Touchstone* 19, no. 5 (June 2006): 24.

in virtue, and leading them to Christ. This is supernatural paternity, the third and highest degree of generation.

Supernatural Fatherhood

The ultimate joy of parents is not simply seeing their children happy on earth; it is seeing them happy forever in heaven. From the perspective of faith, then, transmitting physical life only makes sense if the more perfect moral and spiritual life is also transmitted. As Pope Pius XII observed to parents, "You are, under the direction of the priests, the first and the closest educators and teachers of the children whom God has given to you. In the building of the temple of the Church, which is made not from dead stones but from souls living with new heavenly life, you are the spiritual guides for your children; you yourselves are, as it were, priests of the cradle, infancy and childhood, and you must show them the way to heaven."[16] What a difference it would make in the world if every Christian parent understood this!

Hints of supernatural fatherhood can actually be glimpsed in the structure of natural human generation. No human being, after all, has the power to generate a rational, immortal soul *ex nihilo* ("out of nothing"). Only God can do that. Nevertheless, the fruit of human generation *is* a being with a rational, immortal soul. Astonishing as it is, there is a direct, creative intervention by God *every time* a child is conceived. This is why we say that animals reproduce but, unlike men and women, they do not pro-*create*. It follows that the highest fulfillment of a human child will not simply be in the order of nature—as it would be in the case of an-

---

[16] Pope Pius XII, "Allocution to Married Couples," January 15, 1941.

imals—but in the supernatural order of grace. The unique, creative act of God in the generation of every human child testifies to the supreme responsibility of parents to prepare their children for eternal life.

There is another anticipation of spiritual generation in the transmission of natural life. Parents cannot themselves create a rational soul, but only prepare the physical matter to receive it from God. So too with spiritual generation: parents cannot "create" the life of grace in the souls of their children, but they can, so to speak, prepare the matter of their children's hearts, minds, and souls to receive the gift of grace, the supernatural life that God so earnestly wishes to give them.

This structural resemblance between biological and natural paternity, on the one hand, and supernatural paternity, on the other, hints at other comparisons too. In supernatural generation, Christian parents begin their children on the journey of faith through Baptism, a "new birth" into a life of grace through a sacramental ritual of water that is intended to resemble physical birth. After the spiritual birth of Baptism, parents strive to raise their children in the faith in a way that again parallels the natural development of children. By leading and educating their children in the faith, parents are "the first heralds of the Gospel for their children," by which they "become fully parents, in that they are begetters not only of bodily life but also of the life that through the Spirit's renewal flows from the Cross and Resurrection of Christ," in the words of St. John Paul II.[17] Educating children

---

[17] Pope John Paul II, Apostolic Exhortation on the Role of the Christian Family in the Modern World *Familiaris Consortio* (November 22, 1981) § 39.

in the faith, praying and sacrificing for them, encouraging them in a life of prayer and growth in the theological virtues, and protecting them from spiritual harm, all constitute ways in which parents are supernaturally generative in the lives of their offspring.

Supernatural generation is therefore exercised in a powerful way by natural parents who understand and take this role seriously. However, just as natural paternity can be exercised without biological generation (for example, by adoptive parents, mentors, and teachers), so too can supernatural paternity. In a certain sense, every baptized Christian, certainly every adult Christian, is called to generate supernatural life according to the circumstances of his or her life and vocation. A parish volunteer teaching the faith to children or candidates in RCIA, a woman taking her grandchildren to visit the sick during the holidays, a young man offering sacrifices for those estranged from God, and an aunt fervently praying that her nephews and nieces grow in discipleship are among the countless ways Christians can exercise supernatural generation. Karol Wojtyla (later, Pope John Paul II) saw it as so universal a calling that he identified its exercise as a key sign of a person's spiritual maturity.[18]

Just as fathers and mothers have distinct and complementary roles in biological and natural generation, so too are their roles in supernatural generation distinct and complementary. It should be pointed out, first, that the distinction is not as great as that in natural, let alone biological, parenthood. Nevertheless, the way that the grace of spiritual generativity

---

[18] See Karol Wojtyla, *Love and Responsibility*, trans. H. T. Willetts (New York: Farrar, Straus, Giroux, 1981), 261.

is exercised by men and women does differ and retains the basic pattern of natural generation. The supernatural fatherhood of men retains the features that distinguish their natural fatherhood, and the supernatural motherhood of women retains the features of their natural motherhood. One writer points to the example of Mother Teresa as an image of faithful spiritual motherhood, which in its profound generative fecundity cannot simply be collapsed into a gender-neutral "parenthood." She was supernaturally generative as a *mother*.[19]

Supernatural fatherhood is likewise not exercised androgynously but specifically by a man, and hence his active, initiating, and outward mode of generativity is ordered to fulfilling his role as a supernatural father. As he is to be the provider, guide, and protector of his family, these duties remain his in the supernatural realm as well. He therefore has a particular responsibility to exercise a humble authority in nurturing the life of grace in the souls of his family members.

Sts. Augustine and Chrysostom both identified the family as the "domestic church," a phrase that has emerged again in recent times, with the father as its priest. Augustine no doubt startled his congregation when he once referred to the fathers among them as "my fellow bishops" and told them to be faithful to the duties of their ministry.[20] The father is to

---

[19] See Mary F. Rousseau, "Pope John Paul II's Letter on the Dignity and Vocation of Women: The Call to Communio," *Communio: International Catholic Review* 16, no. 2 (Summer 1989): 219–220.

[20] Cited in Scott Hahn, "The Paternal Order of Priests," in *Spiritual Fatherhood: Living Christ's Own Revelation of the Father. Third Annual Symposium on the Spirituality and Identity of the Diocesan Priest, March 13–16, 2003*, ed. Edward G. Matthews (Emmitsburg, MD: Mount St. Mary's Seminary, 2003), 1. Also see Joseph C. Atkinson, "Paternity in Crisis: Biblical and Philosophical Roots of Fatherhood," *Josephinum Journal of Theology* 9, no. 1 (Winter/Spring 2002): 10.

take the lead in providing his children with opportunities for nourishment in the sacramental life of the Church, in teaching them and guiding them in the faith, and in protecting them against pernicious influences and the wolves who would devour his domestic flock.

Perhaps the most compelling evidence for the distinctive supernatural paternity of the father is his unique responsibility to represent God the Father to his children. It is a fact that most younger children tend to identify God with the characteristics of their father, especially his capacity (or lack thereof) to integrate power with a nurturing love.[21] God has revealed himself as a Father, and it makes sense that human fatherhood is the lens through which most children perceive him. It is "an awesome burden," Professor Janet Smith writes, "on human fathers to realize that they will greatly affect how their children relate to God in virtue of how they perform their role as father."[22] Perhaps this witness value of fatherhood is seen most clearly in its absence, or by its distortion, when so many conceive a false image of God because of absent or inadequate father figures in their lives. Viewed positively, for many fathers it can be a source of encouragement to know that their efforts to be worthy of their vocation will yield tremendous spiritual fruit in the hearts

---

[21] See the interesting study by Jane R. Dickie, Amy K. Eshleman, Dawn M. Merasco, Amy Shepard, Michael Vander Wilt, and Melissa Johnson, "Parent-Child Relationships and Children's Images of God," *Journal for the Scientific Study of Religion* 36, no. 1 (March 1997): 31–32. Joseph Kentenich reflects, for example, on the role of St. Therese's saintly father in her own understanding of God; see Joseph Kentenich, *Rediscovering the Father: Selected Texts for the Year of God the Father* (Mumbai, India: St. Paul Press, 1999), 87–90.

[22] Janet Smith, *The Fatherhood of God* (Denver, CO: Unpublished Manuscript, 2000).

and lives of their children. This latter point is nowhere more true than in the paradigmatic supernatural fatherhood of the Catholic priest.

THE PRIEST'S FATHERHOOD

It is the great privilege of the celibate priest to dedicate his entire life to exercising this third and highest degree of fatherhood: supernatural generation in the order of grace. Certainly, some members of the lay faithful may devote themselves more fully to the exercise of supernatural paternity, even forgoing biological and natural fatherhood entirely, and do so with great fruitfulness. So too some priests may find themselves deeply immersed in the exigencies of natural paternity, engaged, for instance, in the corporal works of mercy or the education of children. The heroic efforts of St. John Vianney, patron saint of parish priests, to feed, shelter, educate, and protect his beloved orphan girls of Providence School, for example, prompted his biographer Abbé Trochu to remark that "surely there never was a better father nor one better loved."[23]

In light of the impoverishment of fatherhood noted earlier, the need for priests to exercise natural paternity may be more urgent today than ever in order to fill the gap left by absent or negligent biological fathers. One Catholic psychologist observes that even brief, regular contact with a strong substitute father, such as a priest, can be of enormous per-

---

[23] Francis Trochu, *The Curé d'Ars: St. Jean-Marie-Baptiste Vianney* (Westminster, MD: The Newman Press, 1949), 209. Catholic priests who are married, of course, also exercise their biological and natural paternity in their own families.

sonal and emotional benefit to children, and especially boys.[24]

Nevertheless, apart from these exceptional circumstances, the grace of Orders is directed primarily to supernatural generation in the order of grace. We will draw from the template of Christ's own fatherhood, which is exercised both as a representative of God the Father and as an instrument of God's paternity. To begin, however, it is worth canvassing the Scriptural and historical evidence for supernatural paternity itself, and especially that of priests.

The Scriptures emphasize in a particular way the spiritual paternity of Abraham as the father of all believers (Gen 15:5–6; Luke 1:73, 16:24; John 8:39, 56; Acts 7:2; Rom 4:1, 9–18; Gal 3:6–9; and many others). Joseph the son of Jacob received the title of "father to Pharaoh" (Gen 45:8) in a spiritual sense. Moses had a relationship of spiritual paternity to Joshua, as Eli did to Samuel and Elijah to Elisha. Moreover, in the Old Testament, spiritual paternity was frequently associated with the priesthood. Professor Scott Hahn argues that even Adam, the first human father, was "a priest who shares in certain divine prerogatives: a divinized creature who, through his holy work, is also a co-creator with God."[25] After the Fall, Adam's priestly work continued in the heads of families and was passed on to first-born sons. When the Old Covenant priesthood was transferred to Aaron and his descendants, the notion of paternity lingered still among the Order of Levites. When a Levite from Bethlehem came to the house of Micah, for instance, Micah pleaded with him,

---

[24] See Paul C. Vitz and Daniel C. Vitz, "Priests and the Importance of Fatherhood," *Homiletic and Pastoral Review* 109, no. 3 (December 2008): 20.

[25] Scott Hahn, *Many Are Called: Rediscovering the Glory of the Priesthood* (New York: Doubleday, 2010), 42.

"Stay with me, and be to me a father and a priest" (Judg 17:10).[26]

Given this Old Testament background, neither the notion of supernatural paternity nor its association with the priesthood was a novelty among the disciples of Jesus. It is true that Jesus was careful never to refer to himself or his apostles as "father" since, as noted earlier, his mission was precisely to reveal the Fatherhood of God. In addition, his caution underscores the source of all paternity in God. No one, not even the Son, is father as God the Father is father. All others are "fathers" only insofar as they share in God's Fatherhood.

Despite these important qualifications, the New Testament offers ample proof that the earliest Christians enjoyed a deep grasp of spiritual paternity among men. St. John calls his disciples his "little children" no fewer than seven times in his first epistle alone.[27] St. Peter calls Mark his son, though Mark is not his natural child (1 Pet 5:13). St. Paul repeatedly uses the language of supernatural paternity to describe his relationship to those he has begotten in Christ. He writes to the Corinthians, for instance, that he intends "to admonish you as my beloved children. For though you have countless guides in Christ, you do not have many fathers. For I became your father in Christ Jesus through the gospel" (1 Cor 4:14–15). Paul calls himself the father of Onesimus, describes his work with the Thessalonians as that of a father with his children, names Timothy and Titus each his "true child in the faith," and even portrays his supernatural generation of the

---

[26] Almost identical words are used again by the Danites in Judg 18:19.

[27] 1 John 2:1, 12, 28; 3:7, 18; 4:4; 5:21. See also 3 John (v.) 4.

Galatians as a painful process of giving birth.[28] Notice here that Paul's actions mirror, in a supernatural way, natural fatherhood. He regards himself as having generated them in the new life of faith, provided for them with good doctrine and ecclesial identity, guided them in moral instruction, and protected them from erroneous teachings. In every sense of the word, St. Paul knew himself to be a spiritual father in the priestly ministry that he received from Christ.

These intuitions among the earliest Christians regarding supernatural fatherhood were further developed in the patristic period. Spiritual paternity was applied most prominently to the desert monks who fathered through their charity, their instruction, and their mercy. It was also used, however, in reference to secular priests and especially bishops. The writings of St. Ignatius of Antioch, the Passion narrative of Sts. Perpetua and Felicity, and the *Didascalia Apostolorum*, among others, all contain explicit references to the supernatural paternity of priests and bishops.[29] Even unbelievers used the term for Christian clergy. St. Polycarp of Smyrna, a disciple of St. John the Apostle, was berated by a mob as "the teacher of Asia, the father of the Christians."[30]

---

[28] Phlm 10; 1 Thess 2:11; 1 Tim 1:2; 2 Tim 2:1–2; Titus 1:4; Gal 4:19. There are identifiable differences between supernatural motherhood and fatherhood, especially in the way that they are exercised, though there is more overlap in supernatural generation than in biological and natural motherhood and fatherhood. Thus it is not surprising that St. Paul uses maternal imagery to describe his work of supernatural generation, even though as a man he is not a supernatural mother but rather a father, as he himself tells the Corinthians.

[29] See Fernando Benicio Felices Sánchez, *La Paternidad Espiritual del Sacerdote: Fundamentos Teológicos de la Fecundidad Apostólica Presbiteral* (San Juan, Puerto Rico: San Juan de Puerto Rico, 2006), 36–41.

[30] Cited in Hahn, *Many Are Called*, 78.

Attributing spiritual paternity to priests occurs in many later patristic writings as well, most prominently in those of Sts. Ambrose, Ephrem, Athanasius, Gregory of Nyssa, Jerome, John Chrysostom, Augustine, and Gregory the Great, as well as in St. Benedict's Rule.[31]

Perhaps due to an increasingly juridical view of Holy Orders, over the following centuries there was less emphasis placed on the paternity of priests and bishops. But it was never entirely lost. Aquinas, for instance, approvingly quotes Origen and Bede in their remarks on the spiritual paternity of priests and he refers to priestly fatherhood in his commentaries on the Pauline epistles, in his discussion of the virtue of piety in the *Summa Theologiae*, and elsewhere. In his *Summa Contra Gentiles*, Aquinas writes that "some propagate and conserve the spiritual life in a spiritual ministry duly, and this belongs to the sacrament of Orders; and some belong to the bodily and spiritual life simultaneously, which takes place in the sacrament of Matrimony."[32] Three centuries later, St. John of Avila resumed the theme, followed by the *Catechism of the Council of Trent* in the sixteenth century, the "French School" of thinkers, such as Sts. John Eudes and Jean-Jacques Olier, in the seventeenth, St. Alphonsus Liguori in the eighteenth, and St. John Bosco in the nineteenth century, who became a beloved—and very intentional— spiritual father to countless abandoned children in nineteenth-century Italy.[33]

---

[31] See Henri De Lubac, *The Motherhood of the Church*, trans. Sergia Englund (San Francisco: Ignatius Press, 1982), 85–91. Also Felices Sánchez, *La Paternidad Espiritual del Sacerdote*, 46–59.

[32] Aquinas, *Summa Contra Gentiles* IV, chap. 58, no. 6.

[33] See Felices Sánchez, *La Paternidad Espiritual del Sacerdote*, 62–78.

The use of the title "Father" for priests has seen a similar resurgence over time in the Latin Church. Beginning in the fourth century, outside the Byzantine world the title "Father" began to be reserved for select metropolitans, such as Rome, Alexandria, and Carthage. By the year 400, the Council of Toledo used the title ("Papa") only for the Bishop of Rome, though sporadically it was still used for other bishops as well.[34] It began to be systematically used again, however, for the mendicant orders in the thirteenth century and, in more recent times, the Anglo-Saxon world has applied the title to all priests, both secular and religious. It became customary first in Ireland, and then largely through the influence of Cardinal Manning it spread to other English-speaking countries.[35]

This re-appropriation of priestly paternity, both in theology and in custom, has seen a remarkable expansion in the twentieth century. The Second Vatican Council, especially in the documents *Lumen Gentium*, *Christus Dominus*, and *Presbyterorum Ordinis*, comments on the fatherhood of priests. Affirmations of priestly fatherhood are commonplace in the teaching, homilies, and writings of every pope in recent times.[36] To take one notable example, as World War II raged

---

[34] See Felices Sánchez, *La Paternidad Espiritual del Sacerdote*, 41.

[35] See Jerome Rono Nyathi, "Priesthood Today and the Crisis of Fatherhood: Fatherlessness in Africa with Special Reference to Zimbabwe" (diss., Pontifical University of Saint Thomas Aquinas, 2002), 49–50. Nyathi points out that it was Cardinal Manning, quoted above, who was particularly responsible in recent times for its application to diocesan as well as religious clergy (p. 50).

[36] See Sánchez, *La Paternidad Espiritual del Sacerdote*, 96–153. Instances of Pope Benedict XVI's and Pope Francis' statements on priestly paternity will be cited in the course of this work.

in Europe, Pope Pius XII delivered a poignant radio message about the urgent need in those troubled days for the spiritual fatherhood of priests. "The parish priest," he said, "is a pastor and a father, a pastor of souls and a spiritual father. We must keep in mind, dear children, that if the work of the Church . . . is not to become sterile, but always life-giving, wholesome, and efficacious, it must focus on ensuring that men can live and die in the grace of God. Instructing the faithful in Christian thought, forming them in discipleship and in the imitation of Christ, paving the narrow way to the kingdom of heaven, and making our environment truly Christian—this is the proper mission of the priest as teacher, father, and pastor of his parish."[37]

That the priest exercises spiritual paternity is important and meaningful, then, if not exactly novel. What has received less attention is how that fatherhood is lived out, a question to which we now turn.

Revealing the Father's Paternity

Jesus represents the Father through his Sacred Humanity, as when he tells St. Philip, "He who has seen me has seen the Father" (John 14:9). Jesus is also an instrument of God's paternity, primarily through his perfect conformity to the Father's will for the supernatural generation and redemption of humanity. So too the priest, configured to Christ the Head, exercises spiritual paternity in these two broad ways: he represents the merciful face of the Father, and instrumentally he generates supernatural life in the souls of his

---

[37] Pope Pius XII, "Discourse of His Holiness Pius XII to the Parish Priests of Rome and the Lenten Preachers," February 6, 1940 (author's translation).

brothers and sisters.

Though all the baptized are to be representatives of God's paternity, particularly through the virtue of charity whereby they reveal the face of the Father to humanity, the priest does so in a unique way through the indelible character of the seal that configures him to act as Christ's representative, and hence as the Father's.

The 2004 *Directory for the Pastoral Ministry of Bishops* teaches that the bishop, in the fullness of Holy Orders, is head of the Church "in the name of the Father, whose image he makes present."[38] That same document explains that the bishop's configuration to Christ renders him a "member of the Church and simultaneously head and shepherd of the Christian people, as brother and as father, as disciple of Christ and teacher of faith, as son of the Church and, in some sense, father of the Church, as minister of the supernatural rebirth of Christians."[39] Though of a lower Order, priests share in this representative role as well. It goes without saying that the priest's disclosure of God's Fatherhood is also evidenced negatively by clergy sexual abuse which causes untold damage to the faith of believers in a loving Father, whose goodness those priests were called to represent.

More directly, however, the priest exercises his fatherhood through his conformity to Christ's redemptive mission, continuing his saving work on earth. This is the "instrumental" paternity of the priest because he generates supernatural life in the souls of believers as an instrument, not as

---

[38] Congregation for Bishops, *Directory for the Pastoral Ministry of Bishops* Apostolorum Successores (Vatican City State: Libreria Editrice Vaticana, 2004), no. 56.

[39] Congregation for Bishops, *Apostolorum Successores*, no. 33.

the source and giver. He is a secondary cause of the Lord's own redemptive work by transmitting life through his identification with Christ the Head of the Church.[40] Certainly only Christ is Head and only he can confer the divine gift of grace. Nevertheless, Christ did confer on his apostles and their successors the power to continue his mission to build up the People of God. Their ministry is subordinate to his, dependent on his, and yet, by divine election, confirmed by him as his agents of redemption. As Christ is the New Adam, the Head of the Church, and thereby its father, so too is the priest, sacramentally conformed to that same Head, truly called a father to Christians.[41]

Though the priest's fatherhood is primarily supernatural, there is even a sense in which it is also physical or "biological" when viewed from the perspective of eternity. Fr. Frederick Miller, theologian and seminary spiritual director, points out that since the priest's spiritual fatherhood is directed to the holiness of his children, and holiness is ordered to salvation and ultimately the resurrection of the body, priestly paternity includes by anticipation a kind of physical generation too. Applying the insight to the life of St. John Vianney, Miller writes that by restoring divine life to souls, Vianney's priestly ministry

> ensured the physical resurrection from the dead on the day of Christ's return in glory. In this sense, the priest's spiritual fatherhood will have an amazing

---

[40] José Granados, "Priesthood: A Sacrament of the Father," *Communio: International Catholic Review* 36, no. 2 (Summer 2009): 208.
[41] See Hahn, "The Paternal Order of Priests," 2.

physical effect on the Last Day. On the day of his funeral, unbelievers surely thought of John Vianney as a lonely old man without progeny, yet tens of thousands of his children attended his funeral and wept for the man who had given them the gift of eternal life in baptism or restored it, when lost through mortal sin, in the sacrament of penance. How many men and women will rise from the grave on the Last Day and enter the Kingdom of Heaven in the flesh because of the ministry of Saint John Vianney? When they meet him, they will call him Father.[42]

The priest does, then, indeed generate new life. He procreates, as it were, in the order of grace. It is a genuine, and not merely metaphorical, paternity. One may object that the priest cannot be a "real" father because he cannot himself generate grace, supernatural life, in the souls of his people. This is certainly true. Only God can do that. That is why the priest's is an instrumental paternity. But as pointed out earlier, this is true of all human fatherhood. Even biological fathers are cooperators with God. Sexual union can prepare the matter, so to speak, but men and women in themselves have no more power to generate human souls on their own than a priest can generate grace. An immortal, rational, human soul can be created by no one but God. God's love enters into a union and makes it fruitful, and the same is true of the priest's ministry. His fatherhood, like all human fatherhood, is instrumental, a cooperation in God's activity, and yet, like biological fatherhood, not less sublime or "real." In fact,

---

[42] Frederick L. Miller, *The Grace of Ars* (San Francisco: Ignatius Press, 2010), 60.

while acknowledging that biological and natural fatherhood remain the basis and template for all human fatherhood, nonetheless, since supernatural generation is the highest degree of human fatherhood, in a certain sense a priest is *more* a father than a natural father; certainly he is not less. One might even argue that if the priest's is not true fatherhood, neither is any other!

Emphasizing the supernatural paternity of priests may seem to weaken the common assertion that the celibate priest is "married" to the Church. After all, it is not Christ as Bridegroom to whom the priest is ontologically conformed but Christ as Head.[43] St. Augustine was in fact reluctant to call the priest the spouse of the Church since it is Christ alone who is her Bridegroom. He preferred the comparison of the priest to St. John the Baptist, the "friend" of the Bridegroom.[44] Nevertheless, there is a sense in which the priest can be said to espouse the Church, since his spiritual fatherhood presupposes the Church's motherhood. In his letter to the Ephesians, for example, St. Paul makes an explicit comparison of the Church to the Bride of Christ. To the Galatians he writes that the Church is the New Jerusalem and refers to her in maternal images (Gal 4:26–27). The Book of Revelation speaks of the "marriage of the Lamb" to a Bride "clothed with fine linen, bright and pure," which the sacred writer identifies with the "righteous deeds of the saints"—that is, of the members of the Church (Rev 19:7–

---

[43] See CCC 1548.

[44] See Andrew Cozzens, "Imago Vivens Iesu Christi Sponsi Ecclesiae: The Priest as a Living Image of Jesus Christ the Bridegroom of the Church through the Evangelical Counsels" (diss., Pontifical University of Saint Thomas Aquinas, 2008), 272–278.

8).[45] A lengthy patristic and theological tradition comments on the same theme. It is precisely through this maternity of the Church that the priest's paternity is fruitful; and, in that sense, he can be called her spouse. Like the first Israel, the family of God that makes up the New Israel is presided over by priest-fathers—the apostles, their successors, and priestly collaborators—as faithful spouses of their chaste Bride.

EXERCISE OF PRIESTLY FATHERHOOD

The Sacrament of Holy Orders, according to the Catechism of the Catholic Church, "configures the recipient to Christ by a special grace of the Holy Spirit, so that he may serve as Christ's instrument for his Church. By ordination one is enabled to act as a representative of Christ, Head of the Church, in his threefold office priest, prophet, and king" (CCC 1581). Since it is the priest's configuration to Christ as Head of the Church that establishes his supernatural fatherhood, it follows that this "threefold office" of sanctification, teaching, and shepherding provide a framework through which to explore the priest's exercise of paternity.

Munus Sanctificandi

The first of these three offices through which a priest exercises fatherhood is the *munus sanctificandi*, or the office of sanctification, which he practices in his priestly ministry and especially in his administration of the sacraments. It must be reiterated that Christ is the primary cause of the

---

[45] See Eph 5:24–27. For example, "the Jerusalem above is free, and she is our mother" (Gal 4:26). See also Rev 3:12 and 21:2, 9.

sacraments while the priest is the instrumental cause—but his causality is no less real for that. The priest truly bestows supernatural life in Baptism, confirms and strengthens it in Confirmation, heals it in Confession and Anointing, and directs it to the common good through Holy Orders and by witnessing Matrimony.[46] It is above all in the Eucharist that the priest objectively exercises his fatherly vocation, since, as the "source and summit" of the Church's life, it is the very source of supernatural generation.

Through the Eucharist the priest "generates" Christ—whose eternal generation by the Father is the prime analogue of all paternity. St. John Eudes wrote that there are three generations of the Son: his eternal generation by the Father, the temporal in the womb of Mary, and the Eucharist by the priest.[47] This source of his paternity also suggests a more personal lesson since it is through a reverent and daily celebration of the Eucharist that the priest touches most closely the font of his own generativity, the eternal and temporal generations of the Son. As Pope John Paul II preached to the Italian clergy in 1984, for the priest

> it is Eucharistic love that daily renews his fatherhood and makes it fruitful, transforming him ever more into Christ and, like Christ, makes him become the bread of souls, their priest, yes, but also their victim, because for them he is gladly consumed in imitation of him who gave his life for the sal-

---

[46] See Pope Pius XI, Encyclical Letter on the Catholic Priesthood *Ad Catholici Sacerdotii* (December 20, 1935), §§ 17–18.

[47] See Felices Sánchez, *La Paternidad Espiritual del Sacerdote*, 70.

vation of the world. In other words, a priest is as good as his Eucharistic life, his Mass above all. A Mass without love, a sterile priest. A fervent Mass, a priest who wins souls.[48]

Through the Mass the priest is confirmed as father, visibly present as Head of the Body, and transformed by grace to live Christ's fruitful sacrifice in his own priestly life. Through it he feeds his people with the Lord's Body and Blood. The celebration of the Eucharist is truly the source and summit not only of the life of the Church but of the priest's supernatural fatherhood as well.

Munus Docendi

The second office is that of teaching and preaching—the *munus docendi*. "The preacher's voice," St. John of the Cross said, must "possess the power to raise a dead man from his sepulcher."[49] Perhaps the great Carmelite's thought could be expressed even more precisely: the preacher's voice *does* possess the power to raise the dead, to give life. Countless stories of conversion begin with the voice of a priest. This aspect of paternity is partly indirect, since it is through preaching and teaching that a priest prepares souls to receive the sacraments, especially Baptism and the Eucharist, which are themselves supernaturally fruitful. The Second Vatican Council taught that non-Christians "are led by the

---

[48] Pope John Paul II, "A Priest is as Good as His Eucharistic Life: Pope to Italian Clergy," February 16, 1984.

[49] St. John of the Cross, "The Ascent of Mount Carmel," book 3, chap. 45, in *The Collected Works of St. John of the Cross*, trans. Kieran Kavanaugh, OCD, and Otilio Rodriguez, OCD (Washington, DC: ICS Publications, 1991), 349.

proclamation of the Gospel to faith and by the saving sacraments," while even in the Christian community "the preaching of the Word is required for the sacramental ministry itself, since the sacraments are sacraments of faith, drawing their origin and nourishment from the Word."[50]

Beyond preparing people to receive the sacraments, however, transmitting the faith is directly generative as well, akin to the teaching function of natural fatherhood. "Sacred doctrine," Aquinas writes, "is food and drink, because it nourishes the soul. For the other sciences only enlighten the soul, but this one enlightens . . . and nourishes and strengthens the soul."[51]

Many people complain that Catholic preaching today is woefully inadequate, and no doubt this is often true and should be addressed. It may be, though, that both preachers and hearers sometimes underestimate the power of the Spirit to draw life even from bland homilies. Preaching can be uninspiring and still inspire. Through preaching, *Lumen Gentium* teaches, the Church "brings forth sons, who are conceived of the Holy Spirit and born of God, to a new and immortal life."[52] Thus, in educating and forming his spiritual children in the faith, a priest exercises his paternity in a powerfully generative way.

It is said that priests "father with their voice," and St. Paul gives us a singular example of this spiritual paternity

[50] Vatican II Council, Decree on the Ministry and Life of Priests *Presbyterorum Ordinis* (December 7, 1965), § 4.

[51] St. Thomas Aquinas, *Super Epistolam ad Hebraeos* (Rome: Marietti, 1953), 5, lec. 2.

[52] Vatican II Council, Dogmatic Constitution on the Church *Lumen Gentium* (November 21, 1964), § 64.

in his first letter to the Corinthians, as cited earlier. "For though you have countless guides in Christ," Paul writes, "you do not have many fathers. For I became your father in Christ Jesus through [preaching] the gospel" (1 Cor 4:15). Sometimes this teaching is even, in a way, physically generative. I know married couples who attribute the very existence of one or more of their children to a priest's sermon on contraception. In one case, they even named two children after him!

The office of preaching will at times come at a personal cost to the priest, since clear and unadulterated preaching is not always a welcome word. No matter how carefully and sensitively the homily is crafted, every faithful priest has experienced rejection after preaching a difficult message. Nevertheless, only courageous and clear preaching will feed his children with the full nourishment of the Gospel. A good father's teaching is sympathetic but also objective and strong, even when it might cause pain, sadness, or anger in his children for a while.

Teaching is one of the ways that the priest infuses, so to speak, the Church with Gospel truths. Indeed it is not too strong to suggest that withholding that teaching is a kind of spiritual contraception, suppressing his own supernatural fecundity with which he is called to build up the Body of Christ. Archbishop Charles Chaput reminds priests that there is "nothing 'pastoral' about keeping quiet in the face of evil. It's not charity to let anyone persist in serious sin, or to help people make excuses. God has entrusted his own children to you. He has given you a share in the authority that his Son alone possessed."[53] Faithfully exercising that authority in forming one's people in the truth of the Gospel is one of the most demanding, and yet rewarding, generative roles of a priest.

Munus Regendi

Thirdly, the priest exercises his paternity through the *munus regendi*, the office of shepherding or ruling. This office is comparable to the "natural" paternity identified earlier in the father's role as provider, guide, and protector. The priest provides for his people primarily by administering the sacraments, above all the Bread of Life, the spiritual food for the children of God. He also provides for his people spiritually through his priestly intercession in prayer. The desert fathers had a keen understanding of this paternal function of intercession, and it has been well preserved in the monastic tradition. Orthodox theologian Kallistos Ware recalls the visit of an American to an elder on Mount Athos. The American asked the monk at the end of their conversation if he might write to ask for further advice. "No," the monk replied, "don't write; but I will pray for you." Ware recounts the disappointment of his friend until another monk, having overheard the conversation, remarked to him, "You ought to be very happy that the *geronta* promised to pray for you. He doesn't say that to everyone. His advice is good, but his prayers are far, far better."[54]

[53] Charles J. Chaput, "The Men He Intended: Claiming Our Vocations as Priests of Jesus Christ," accessed October 5, 2018, https://www.catholicculture.org/culture/library/view.cfm?id=7763.

[54] Kallistos Ware, *The Spiritual Father in St. John Climacus and St. Symeon the New Theologian* (Kalamazoo, MI: Cistercian Publications, 1989), 303.

The priest also spiritually provides for his people through his own sacrifices, as a natural father provides for his children through personal sacrifice. It is incumbent upon a priest to have a vibrant ascetical life and a habit of personal mortification. These mortifications can be small renunciations throughout the day, offered for the needs of his people and his own needs. They should also include more substantial mortifications, including fasting and other corporal mortifications, the fruitfulness of which is confirmed by the testimony of countless saints throughout the ages.

A new kind of sacrifice has presented itself today to priests in many parts of the world when they must live under a pall of undeserved suspicion because of the egregious sexual sins committed by their brother priests. Every priest certainly has a right (and usually a duty, for the sake of his flock) to protect his good name and deny false accusations. More commonly, though, it is not false accusations that priests must bear but simply an unspoken mistrust directed at all priests. For a man who has embraced the priesthood in order to lay down his life for others, being under that cloud of suspicion is a suffering indeed, however priestly and Christlike it is to suffer for the sins of others. It is a sacrifice that, when offered willingly to the Lord, can yield tremendous graces for his people and for himself.

In addition to providing for his children through the sacraments, prayer, and personal sacrifice, a priest is a guide and teacher to his flock through his preaching and catechetical instruction. This is done not only with words. Sometimes his most powerful sermon is his witness to God's paternal love. A faithful priest's heart is dilated with compassion for his people, a deep and authentic sympathy, especially when they are suffering. The concerns of his children are his concerns; their burdens are his burdens; their joys are his joys. With the discernment of a father, he will know when to console, when to encourage, and when to correct. Sharing in the universal mission of the Church, the priest is imbued with a love without boundaries. Within this breadth of love, a priest will reserve a special share of his paternal affection for those most in need of it: the poor, young people, the sick and dying and abandoned, priests and religious, and married couples and families.

When one of his flock strays, he will spare no effort to restore him to grace, and in his reconciliation the priest will be a powerful witness to the merciful forgiveness and love of God. St. John of Avila, a sixteenth-century author who spoke and wrote extensively on the priesthood, writes movingly of his constant and often heart-rending struggle for the souls of his children, with tears and ceaseless vigilance, and when one of them is lost, "there is no suffering to which it compares. I do not believe," says the saint, "that God has left any manner of martyrdom so sorrowful in this world as the torment of the death of a child in the heart of him who is truly his father."[55] There is no more eloquent proof of a priest's fatherly heart than the anguish he experiences in losing one of the "little ones" entrusted to his care.

Spiritual paternity knows nothing of "official" clerical relationships. The priest is ordained to reflect the Father's love not abstractly, not generically, but individually, in im-

---

[55] Juan de Avila, "Carta 1: A Un Predicador," in *Obras Completas Del Santo Maestro Juan de Avila*, ed. Francisco Martin Hernandez, vol. 5 (Madrid, Spain: Biblioteca de Autores Cristianos, 1970), 21, author's translation.

itation of God's personal love for human beings. Not only in his ordinary pastoral ministry, then, but in the chance encounters of every day, the priest can find ways to reveal his paternal love.

As with any good father, a priest guides and teaches his children in such a way that they grow toward a healthy autonomy and the mature freedom of children of God, free especially from false and disordered dependencies. True *paternity* is diametrically opposed to the *paternalism* that keeps children dependent and immature. As in the natural realm where good parents will raise their children to become strong and free adults, able themselves to be generous fathers and mothers, so too in the realm of grace. Good supernatural fathers form their children to become mature Christians, able to assume the duties that they will fulfill in their Christian vocation, whether clerical, religious, or lay, and with their own proper autonomy. Like the best Christian fathers, the priest ultimately does not raise up co-dependent "children" but brothers and sisters in Christ, heirs with him of the Kingdom prepared by the Lord, in which the only hierarchy will be that of sanctity.

Such a vision of paternity demands humility and detachment on the part of the priest. His paternity is always a derived paternity, and hence his children are in the end not *his* children but God's. The priest must therefore always be vigilant to maintain a healthy detachment from any desire to control or manipulate those entrusted to his care. In particular, as a father the priest will resist any temptation to utilize his ministry to fulfill his own emotional needs. We can at times, like all people, become attached to those we serve. Priestly ministry calls for a certain magnanimity and freedom of spirit, the ability to give ourselves generously to those entrusted to our care without expecting anything in return.

Finally, a priest exercises the *munus regendi* as the family protector, a duty directed like a natural father both internally and externally. Internally, the priest's protective function includes the responsibility to exhort and correct his spiritual children when necessary. Though this includes the preaching and teaching of the *munus docendi*, particularly of moral truths, it also encompasses the more formal role of setting familial as well as juridical boundaries for behavior and the practical running of his parish. Exercising this aspect of paternity is not easy. Archbishop Paul Coakley notes that there can be a temptation on the part of many fathers to "seek to win their children's favor by trading on what money can buy, or abdicating their authority in favor of a less demanding and more ingratiating arrangement with their children. Priests as spiritual fathers can make the same mistake."[56]

When a vocal minority tries to railroad an agenda through the parish council, for instance, it is the pastor who ensures that other members are not cowed into silence. When a parish employee undermines the parochial mission through gossip or detraction, it is the pastor who must step in. When parishioners are tempted to "ally" themselves with one priest against another, it is up to the priests to ensure that the spirits of envy and division do not compromise the unity of the parish. Perhaps many priests shy away from this aspect of their paternity because of the legitimate reluctance to adopt

[56] Paul S. Coakley, "The Priest as Father 101," in *Spiritual Fatherhood: Living Christ's Own Revelation of the Father. Third Annual Symposium on the Spirituality and Identity of the Diocesan Priest, March 13–16, 2003*, ed. Edward G. Matthews (Emmitsburg, MD: Mount St. Mary's Seminary, 2003), 38.

the heavy-handed, even capricious, approach that sometimes characterized priestly authority in the past. Priests are ministers of God, not masters of his people, and their authority should be exercised with gentleness, humility, and compassion. A priest is both a father and a brother to his fellow Christians. Nevertheless, precisely as a minister of God, it remains the priest's responsibility to faithfully represent him in exhorting and correcting others when necessary.

Externally, a priest exercises his protective role as spiritual father by defending the faith and the faithful with his words and actions. At times a priest-father must assume a more confrontational approach when doctrinal errors and moral dangers threaten his flock. Many of the great heresies that confronted the Church through the centuries, especially derivatives of Gnosticism, such as Manichaeism and Catharism, were actually imports from the wider culture. They endangered the integrity of the faith and led many astray. Today, external doctrinal threats tend to be more anthropological, such as confusion and dissent about the nature and dignity of man, sexuality, gender, marriage, and family. These errors—which are simply more offshoots of Gnosticism—are causing great harm in the Church and in the world. They are drawing many souls away from God. Indeed these cultural divides are also triggering more explicit external threats to the Church, as in recent encroachments against religious liberty and efforts by secularist governments to restrict religious activities to private worship alone. Courageous priests must continue to be on the front lines of these cultural battles, whatever the personal cost.

Priests are at the forefront of the cosmic spiritual struggle and have been given weapons with which to confront the "enormity of evil" and to encourage and strengthen the people of God so that "the soldiers of Christ can live to fight another day," in the words of Scott Hahn.[57] The priest must be ready to defend the faith against errors that may seduce his people and their families and to counteract those errors with his prayers, sacrifices, and a compelling and bracing vision of Catholicism. At the conclusion to the Year for Priests, Pope Benedict XVI spoke about this difficult service of protective love:

> The shepherd needs the rod as protection against savage beasts ready to pounce on the flock; against robbers looking for prey. Along with the rod there is the staff which gives support and helps to make difficult crossings. Both of these are likewise part of the Church's ministry, of the priest's ministry. The Church too must use the shepherd's rod, the rod with which he protects the faith against those who falsify it, against currents which lead the flock astray. The use of the rod can actually be a service of love. Today we can see that it has nothing to do with love when conduct unworthy of the priestly life is tolerated. Nor does it have to do with love if heresy is allowed to spread and the faith twisted and chipped away, as if it were something that we ourselves had invented. . . . Even so, the rod must always become once again the shepherd's staff—a staff which helps men and women to tread difficult

---

[57] Hahn, *Many Are Called*, 92, 95.

paths and to follow the Lord.[58]

It is in times of such trial that a faithful priest shows himself to be not a hireling but a true shepherd. Like Moses, he is called to stand in the breach, placing himself, like the Good Shepherd, between his people and any danger that may threaten them, defending them from error and confusion within and from threats without, even, if necessary, at the cost of his own life.

The priest's fatherhood, then, is not simply a detached conclusion of theology but the substance and lived experience of every priest's life. It shares in the Fatherhood of God and, like all human fatherhood, fulfills man's universal calling to give life and to foster that new life toward maturity. The priest's ministry, in fact, is ordered to the highest degree of human fatherhood, supernatural paternity in the order of grace. Through his conformity to Christ the Head, the priest is able to exercise it in the threefold *munera* of sanctifier, teacher, and shepherd. This fatherhood is the joy and privilege of every priest, an objective to which he can direct his life, every day. Bearing in mind that vision of priestly fatherhood, we can now consider the role of celibacy in living it out.

---

[58] Pope Benedict XVI, "In Priests the Audacity of a God Close to Us: Mass in St. Peter's Square for Conclusion of the Year for Priests," June 11, 2010.

———— Chapter Two ————

Priestly Celibacy

IN THE BOOK OF GENESIS, when the great patriarch Abram was still childless, the Lord took him outside and said, "'Look toward heaven, and number the stars, if you are able to number them.' . . . 'So shall your descendants be.' And he believed the LORD; and he reckoned it to him as righteousness" (Gen 15:5–6).

Abram strikes a beautiful image of the celibate priest who, though apparently childless, is called to generate innumerable children in the Lord. But there is another feature of this story, pointed out by Scripture scholars, that we sometimes miss. We usually picture Abram going outside, looking up into the night sky and seeing the ocean of stars, and being unable to "number them" because of their vast number. Six verses later, however, we read that "the sun was going down." It was broad daylight when Abram looked up at the sky, and that is why he could not count the stars—because he could not see them. His faith, which was credited to him as righteousness, was the faith of knowing that God would produce from him countless children—children that he could not yet see. He could not see the stars with the eyes of his body, but he could see his children with the eyes of his soul.

In this powerful image of the fruitfulness of celibacy, born of faith, we can begin to envision more clearly the gift of celibate priestly fatherhood.

CELIBACY AND SUPERNATURAL FATHERHOOD

In his 1935 encyclical entitled *Ad Catholici Sacerdotii*, Pope Pius XI quotes a poem by St. Ephrem to a bishop named Abraham:

> Thou art true to thy name, Abraham,
> for thou also art the father of many:
> but because thou hast no wife as Abraham had Sara,
> behold thy flock is thy spouse.
> Bring up its children in thy truth;
> may they become to thee children of the spirit
> and sons of the promise
> that makes them heirs to Eden.[1]

Pius XI was alluding to an ancient understanding of apostolic celibacy as ordered to supernatural generation, the roots of which can be found in the Old Testament treatment of fertility, sterility, and virginity and their fulfillment in the New Covenant. Beginning with God's command to Adam and Eve to "Be fruitful and multiply" (Gen 1:28), the assurance of offspring constituted one of the key indicators of a divine covenant, particularly with the promise of a future Messiah,

---

[1] Pope Pius XI, Encyclical Letter on the Catholic Priesthood *Ad Catholici Sacerdotii* (December 20, 1935), § 44.

among the descendants of Israel. Before Christ, sterility was therefore seen either as a curse or as a condition for God to reveal his power by transforming it into fruitfulness. Thus, to return to the example of Abram, a Hebrew name meaning "Exalted Father," the patriarch was still childless at the age of a hundred when he received an even more incongruous name: *Abraham*, meaning "Father of a Multitude of Nations." As Scott Hahn observes, for a man of Abraham's age without progeny, such a name must have provoked ridicule. "I'm sure the new name didn't make life any easier for old Abraham," Hahn remarks, "as he made his way past the cruelest of his gossipy neighbors."[2]

In time, though, God's promise was fulfilled and Abraham's physical and spiritual descendants did indeed flourish, even to our own day—even to us. Through God's power, Abraham's human sterility was charged with awesome fecundity, both natural and supernatural, and hence became an Old Testament trope that anticipates the fruitfulness of virginity in the New Covenant.

The first line of the New Testament, in fact, is a reference to the fruitfulness of Abraham. Jesus is called the "son of Abraham," and by drawing to himself all the nations, Jew and Gentile alike, God fulfills his promise to Abraham and affirms the literal truth of his name. "Fruitful sterility" is therefore transformed in the New Testament into a "fruitful virginity," consciously chosen, beginning with the virginity of Mary, Joseph, John the Baptist, and, above all, Jesus himself. One theologian identifies this shift in focus from the

---

[2] Scott Hahn, *Many Are Called: Rediscovering the Glory of the Priesthood* (New York: Doubleday, 2010), 123.

fruitfulness of the flesh to the fruitfulness of the spirit as one of the key "turning points" in salvation history.[3]

In the Old Testament, Aquinas argues, it was necessary that the faithful generate physically in order to usher in the Messianic Age. "The counsel of practicing perpetual continence," he continues, was therefore "reserved to the New Testament, when the faithful are multiplied by a spiritual generation."[4] Thus when Jesus extols those who "have made themselves eunuchs for the sake of the kingdom of heaven" and declares that he "who is able to receive this, let him receive it" (Matt 19:12), he is emphasizing its supernatural end, its fecundity in spiritual generation. Indeed, some verses later, Jesus affirms that those who have "left houses or brothers or sisters or father or mother or children or lands, for my name's sake, will receive a hundredfold, and inherit eternal life" (Matt 19:29)[5]—a "hundredfold," which some authors attribute to the superabundant fruitfulness of virginal generativity.[6]

It should be acknowledged that this scriptural support for the supernatural fruitfulness of celibacy is not a direct link to priestly ministry itself, as non-Catholic apologists

---

[3] See Thomas McGovern, *Priestly Identity: A Study in the Theology of Priesthood* (Dublin, Ireland: Four Courts Press, 2002), 102.

[4] Thomas Aquinas, *On the Truth of the Catholic Faith (Summa Contra Gentiles) Book III: Providence*, trans. Vernon J. Bourke (New York: Hanover House, 1955), III, chap. 136, no. 15.

[5] It is interesting that in the Lucan parallel passages to this Matthean text (Luke 18:29), leaving one's "wife" is also included in the list, as if to emphasize in the two renditions that celibacy means giving up both wife and children in the natural order, but receiving them again in the "hundredfold" even in this life (also see Mark 10:29).

[6] See Réginald Garrigou-Lagrange, "La Virginité Consacrée à Dieu: Selon Saint Thomas," *Vie Spirituelle* 10 (1924): 537–538. Also, Jean Galot, "La Motivation Évangélique du Célibat," *Gregorianum* 53, no. 4 (1972): 747.

readily point out. Neither do other Scriptural passages often cited in defense of celibacy include explicit references to ministry—for instance, St. Paul's counsel to the Corinthians that "it is well" for the unmarried and widows "to remain single as I do" (1 Cor 7:8). Indeed, St. Paul's injunctions to both Timothy and Titus that a bishop should be a "husband of one wife" (1 Tim 3:2; Titus 1:6) are often mentioned as definitive proof that ministry was not associated with celibacy in the apostolic age. Nonetheless, while conceding that the Church developed her understanding of celibate priesthood over time, it is by no means clear that these texts rule out early Christian adoption of ministerial celibacy or perpetual continence. After all, St. Paul also insists that a *widow* receiving Church support be the "wife of one husband" (1 Tim 5:9). Clearly, since she is a widow, St. Paul obviously cannot mean that she is currently married but rather that she has renounced any opportunity to marry again. Thus, St. Paul's statements about bishops and deacons likely refer to their renunciation of remarriage if they are, or become, widowed.[7] This, at any rate, was the Church's interpretation of these passages at least from the time of Pope Siricius (fourth century) until modern times.[8] What can be said definitively is that the ambiguous texts of St. Paul do not

---

[7] See Stanley L. Jaki, "Man of One Wife or Celibacy," *Homiletic and Pastoral Review* 86, no. 4 (January 1986): 18–20. Also J. Francis Stafford, "The Eucharistic Foundations of Sacerdotal Celibacy," *Origins* 23, no. 12 (September 2, 1993): 213. A helpful synopsis of the various theories pertaining to the "husband of one wife" label can be found in Joseph T. Lienhard, "Origins and Practice of Priestly Celibacy in the Early Church," in *The Charism of Priestly Celibacy: Biblical, Theological, and Pastoral Reflections*, ed. John C. Cavadini (Notre Dame, IL: Ave Maria Press, 2012), 51–53.

[8] See Pope Paul VI, Encyclical Letter on the Celibacy of the Priest *Sacerdotalis Caelibatus* (June 24, 1967), §§ 21–22.

contradict his other clear statements to the Corinthians about the value of celibacy or the celibate witness and teaching of Jesus himself. They may even reinforce the historical claim that in the early Church perpetual continence was likely the norm for priests, including those married at the time of their ordination.

The practice of clerical celibacy grew rather than declined in the early centuries of the Church. The Council of Elvira (305) in Spain, for example, ratifying what was already an ancient practice, obliged complete continence for bishops, priests, and deacons. Synods, local councils, papal decrees, and even penitential books over the following centuries did the same. The Second Lateran Council (1139)—often erroneously cited as the beginning of obligatory celibacy for priests— merely restated, in response to rampant abuses, what had long been the practice of the Latin Church and declared invalid any marriage contracted by a cleric. The Eastern Church did not hold as stringently to the apostolic norm, though even in the Eastern Churches, for whom the Council of Trullo (691) permitted married clergy, ordination remained an impediment to marriage and the celibate norm was (and still is) maintained for bishops who possess the fullness of Holy Orders.[9]

The sense of the suitability of priestly celibacy continued to deepen through the centuries. Jean Galot writes that this appreciation required

---

[9] For more detail on the history of celibacy see, for instance, Stefan Heid, *Celibacy in the Early Church: The Beginnings of Obligatory Continence for Clerics in East and West* (San Francisco: Ignatius Press, 2001). Also, Christian Cochini, *The Apostolic Origins of Priestly Celibacy* (San Francisco: Ignatius Press, 1990).

a whole historical evolution. The remarkable fact in this evolution is that the exalted ideal of celibacy continued to gain strength in spite of a human nature slanted in the opposite direction. Severe crises occurred. In certain periods, the fifteenth century in particular, the majority of clerics transgressed the law, so much so that the abrogation of it was pleaded for. But the law was upheld, and the authority of the Church took pains to devise means to insure a better compliance with it. In this supernatural ascent, we must recognize the Holy Spirit at work: he imparts an ever keener understanding and an ever better realization of what the gospel calls the priesthood to be.[10]

Through the years, the association of priestly celibacy with supernatural generativity was never entirely lost, though it did ebb and flow. The writings of early Christian authors—such as Origen, Pseudo-Jerome, Sts. Ephrem, Damasus, and Gregory the Great, and particularly Eusebius of Caesarea—make the point explicitly, as did later writers.[11] The eleventh-century St. Peter Damian, for example, emphasized that the bishop's celibacy reflects his "marriage" to the local Church, represented by the episcopal ring that Damian likened to a wedding ring.[12]

---

[10] Jean Galot, *Theology of the Priesthood*, trans. Roger Balducelli (San Francisco: Ignatius Press, 1984), 242.

[11] See, for instance, Laurent Touze, "Paternidad Divina y Paternidad Sacerdotal," *XX Simposio Internacional de Teología de la Universidad de Navarra* (Pamplona, Spain: Servicio de Publicaciones de la Universidad de Navarra, 2000), 656–662. Also, Stanley L. Jaki, *Theology of Priestly Celibacy* (Front Royal, VA: Christendom, 1997), 79.

[12] See Touze, "Paternidad Divina y Paternidad Sacerdotal," 661.

In recent times the relationship between priestly celibacy and spiritual fatherhood has begun to emerge again more forcefully. Pope Pius XII, for instance, in his Apostolic Exhortation *Menti Nostrae*, drawing together the thought of Sts. Ambrose, John of Avila, Alphonsus Liguori, and John Bosco, taught that by the law of celibacy, "the priest, so far from losing the gift and duties of fatherhood, rather increases them immeasurably, for, although he does not beget progeny for this passing life of earth, he begets children for that life which is heavenly and eternal."[13]

The Second Vatican Council's *Decree on the Ministry and Life of Priests* describes celibacy as "a source of spiritual fruitfulness in the world" and renders priests "better fitted for a broader acceptance of fatherhood in Christ."[14] Similarly, St. Paul VI, in his encyclical *Sacerdotalis Caelibatus*, remarks that the priest's celibacy "inculcates in him, as a sign of a higher and greater fatherhood, a generosity and refinement of heart which offer a superlative enrichment."[15] St. John Paul II makes explicit the connection between celibacy and spiritual fatherhood in his Apostolic Exhortation *Familiaris Consortio*, in which he reminds the Church that, "in spite of having renounced physical fecundity, the celibate person becomes spiritually fruitful, the father and mother of many,

---

[13] Pope Pius XII, Apostolic Exhortation on the Development of Holiness in Priestly Life *Menti Nostrae* (September 23, 1950), § 20. Also see Fernando Benicio Felices Sánchez, *La Paternidad Espiritual del Sacerdote: Fundamentos Teológicos de la Fecundidad Apostólica Presbiteral* (San Juan, Puerto Rico: San Juan de Puerto Rico, 2006), 99.

[14] Vatican II Council, Decree on the Ministry and Life of Priests *Presbyterorum Ordinis* (December 7, 1965), § 16.

[15] Pope Paul VI, *Sacerdotalis Caelibatus*, § 56.

cooperating in the realization of the family according to God's plan."[16]

Revealing God's Fatherhood

The priest, as stated earlier, is conformed to Jesus the Head of the Church. He both represents God's paternity and generates new life in the order of grace. Celibacy is a privileged way of living both aspects of his fatherhood.

With respect to the first, representing God's own Fatherhood, celibacy is manifestly a closer approximation to the paternity of the Father. Early authors such as Sts. Gregory of Nyssa and Gregory Nazianzen reflect on the "virginal generation" within the Trinity, both in the absence of a sexual component and in its spiritual purity and freedom from passion.[17] As French theologian Louis Bouyer writes, citing St. Gregory of Nyssa, "Divine fatherhood, the only true fatherhood worthy of the name, is essentially virginal."[18] This primordial normativity of celibate generativity is found in the virginal generation of the Eternal Son and in the virginal generation of the Church by the celibate Incarnate Son.[19]

---

[16] See Pope John Paul II, Apostolic Exhortation on the Role of the Christian Family in the Modern World *Familiaris Consortio* (November 22, 1981), § 16.

[17] See Verna Harrison, "Gender, Generation, and Virginity in Cappadocian Theology," *Journal of Theological Studies* 47, no. 1 (April 1996): 45–46.

[18] Louis Bouyer, *Woman in the Church*, trans. Marilyn Teichert (San Francisco: Ignatius Press, 1979), 33.

[19] Though it is no longer taken for granted everywhere that Jesus remained unmarried and virginal, it will be presumed for the purposes of this book. One may consult the overview of Christ's virginity in Allen H. Vigneron, "Christ's Virginal Heart and His Priestly Charity," in *Chaste celibacy: living Christ's own spousal love: Sixth Annual Symposium on the Spirituality and Identity of the Diocesan Priest, March 15–18, 2007* (Omaha, NE: The Institute for Priestly Formation, 2007). Archbishop Vigneron's talk includes a brief survey of the

Celibate priestly fatherhood therefore reveals the Father-hood of God in a particularly striking way. Celibacy reflects the inner logic of divine paternity as the priest stands in the place of the celibate Christ who reveals the "celibate" Father and generates in a celibate way. Celibate priests possess a unique capacity, then, to reveal the Father and the Father's love, a representation that is somewhat diminished in the case of a married priest who must reserve a privileged share of that paternal love for his natural family.

Even more concretely than this representative pater-nity, however, the instrumental paternity of the priest is reinforced by his celibate commitment. Christ's paternity is instrumental insofar as his Sacred Humanity generates supernatural life as an agent of redemption, as both Head and Bridegroom of the Church. The priest, conformed to Christ the Head, shares in this divine paternity. Since Je-sus' Sacred Humanity was ordered in every respect to his redemptive mission, it follows that his choice of celibacy,

current state of the question. He speculates that one reason why so many today have subscribed to the hypothesis that Jesus had a sexual relation-ship with Mary Magdalene is because "a nuptial relationship with a woman disciple would bleach out the eschatological dimension of Christ's life and ministry, and that disappearance would be welcome news to someone who has lost confidence in the eschaton. In such a perspective, Christ's Pasch would be left as a tragic accident that befell a decent 'family man' and took him from his home before his time. In other words, Christ's possession of a spousal relationship with a woman disciple would tame him; quite literally, it would 'domesticate' him. And the further consequences would be that the Church should be understood as in intra-worldly institution, not as a transcended mystery, and the Christian life understood as citizenship in the earthly city not citizenship in the Jerusalem from on high." Also see Allen H. Vigneron, "The Virginity of Jesus and the Celibacy of His Priests," in *The Charism of Priestly Celibacy: Biblical, Theological, and Pastoral Reflections*, ed. John C. Cavadini (Notre Dame, IL: Ave Maria Press, 2012).

like that of the priest, is likewise ordered to that same supernatural generativity. As author and seminary formator Fr. Gary Selin writes, "Christ, the mediator between heaven and earth by virtue of the Incarnation, lived his life in the state of celibacy, which witnesses to his total dedication to the service of God and humankind. It is fitting, therefore, that the ministerial priest, who is called by Christ to follow him wherever he goes, should be celibate and should live his priesthood with a heart full of pastoral charity."[20] The Congregation for Education states it succinctly: "Priestly celibacy is a communion in the celibacy of Christ."[21]

That Christ's celibacy was a fitting accompaniment to his redemptive mission, by the way, does not imply that Jesus was unable to marry. To suggest that marriage was impossible or unbecoming for Jesus is tantamount to saying either that he was not fully human or that there is something sinful or shameful in matrimony or conjugal love, since it is only in sinlessness that Jesus' humanity is distinguished. Galot dryly observes that considering marriage "unworthy of the incarnate Word betrays a rather low estimation of marriage."[22] And yet, Galot continues, it "was appropriate that he who was inaugurating the spiritual engendering of a new humanity should abstain from bodily engendering. For him, fecundity and offspring would be in the order of grace."[23] Jesus was the New Adam, the Head of a redeemed

---

[20] Gary Selin, *Priestly Celibacy: Theological Foundations* (Washington, DC: The Catholic University of America Press, 2016), 115.

[21] Congregation for Catholic Education, "Formation in Celibacy," *Origins* 4, no. 5 (June 27, 1974): 70, no. 14.

[22] Galot, *Theology of the Priesthood*, 230.

[23] Galot, *Theology of the Priesthood*, 230.

humanity, and the new life he inaugurated is not generation in the flesh but supernatural generation. It was fitting that it be initiated by a virginal father. Stated differently, if Christ had elected to marry and conceive natural children, the symbolic power of his generativity in grace would have been radically diminished.

Moreover, Christ's celibacy reflected a complete openness to the Father's will. St. Paul VI taught that Christ's celibacy "signified His total dedication to the service of God and men. This deep concern between celibacy and the priesthood of Christ is reflected in those whose fortune it is to share in the dignity and mission of the Mediator and eternal Priest."[24] Christ's celibacy is therefore ordered to the Father's salvific will, to the universal love of those whom the Father has given him. The particular bond of affection and responsibility in marriage, holy and beautiful in its own right, would have been out of place in his all-embracing mission. His was to be a universal supernatural paternity as the New Adam, the father of a spiritual family without bounds, and given the particular responsibilities that marriage would have imposed, Galot contends, "Jesus firmly frees himself from these constraints for the sake of a wider orientation."[25]

Far from excluding human affection, then, the priest's celibacy is ordered, like that of Jesus, to an unbounded love that broadens the heart and frees him for a broader ministry. That is, the fittingness of the priest's celibacy mirrors the fittingness of Christ's. Galot writes that the "priestly

---

[24] Pope Paul VI, *Sacerdotalis Caelibatus*, § 21. Also see Congregation for the Clergy, *Directory for the Life and Ministry of Priests*, no. 81.

[25] Galot, *Theology of the Priesthood*, 231.

mission of Christ did make it appropriate that he should renounce a family of his own; it did not make this renunciation
necessary. In this appropriateness lies the reason why celibacy is appropriate for a priesthood exercised in the name of
Christ."[26] The supernatural fecundity of Christ in the order
of redemption is reflected on the part of his ministers by
their wholehearted dedication to supernatural fruitfulness.
Priestly celibacy emphasizes the fact that such fruitfulness
can only come from God in the order of grace.

Perhaps the overwhelming support for priestly celibacy voiced by most priests reflects their intuition that it is
uniquely suited to one engaged in pastoral ministry. The
priesthood is fundamentally a gift of oneself for the good
of others, and it is most fittingly accompanied by the radical self-gift represented by celibacy. There is a harmony,
in other words, between priestly celibacy and the mode of
generation that the priest exercises as a man sacramentally
configured to Christ the Head of the Church. "By a life of
celibate chastity," Archbishop Allen Vigneron writes, "the
man who shares in and makes present the priesthood of
Christ the Head more deeply participates in and more clearly presents this total virginal self-giving of Jesus, which is
the essence and foundation of his priesthood. Put simply, a
celibate priest is more like Christ the High Priest, and so is
and acts in ways that are more intensely priestly."[27]

Since the priest's ministry is exercised in and through
the Church, his celibacy is a fitting counterpart to the
Church's virginal motherhood. Conformed to Christ, the

---

[26] Galot, *Theology of the Priesthood*, 244.
[27] Vigneron, "The Virginity of Jesus and the Celibacy of His Priests," 98.

celibate priest enjoys the honor of imitating the Lord's undivided and fruitful love for his virginal Spouse. In recent years the Church has often pointed out this aspect of celibacy. The Second Vatican Council taught that through celibacy priests profess "their willingness to be dedicated with undivided loyalty to the task entrusted to them, namely that of espousing the faithful to one husband and presenting them as a chaste virgin to Christ. They recall that mystical marriage, established by God and destined to be fully revealed in the future, by which the Church holds Christ as her only spouse."[28] In the words of *Pastores Dabo Vobis*, the "Church, as the spouse of Jesus Christ, wishes to be loved by the priest in the total and exclusive manner in which Jesus Christ her head and spouse loved her."[29] Thus, celibacy is ordered to the priest's fruitful spousal love of the Church, the virginal mother through whom his paternity is revealed, confirmed, and made effective. He becomes an image of the exclusive love of Christ for his Bride, and imitating the divine Bridegroom, he commits himself to loving her generously, with his whole heart.

There was for Christ, as there is for every priest, a sacrificial dimension of celibacy that echoes the sacrifice of the life-giving Paschal Mystery. As mentioned earlier, it is not irreverent to suggest that forgoing marriage was a sacrifice for Christ; indeed the irreverence would be in suggesting that his human nature was incapable of desiring the individuated love of marriage and children, or in suggesting

---

[28] Vatican II Council, *Presbyterorum Ordinis*, § 16.

[29] Pope John Paul II, Post-Synodal Apostolic Exhortation on the Formation of Priests in the Circumstances of the Present Day *Pastores Dabo Vobis* (March 15, 1992), § 29.

that marriage was unworthy of his desire. Therefore, while Christ's celibacy was ordered primarily to his undivided and universal love for God and man, it also included a sacrifice that was supernaturally generative, a preparation and a glimpse of the fruitfulness of Calvary.

Celibate priests share in this life-giving sacrifice. The legitimate longings for a woman's companionship and the joys of a family are an invitation to the celibate priest to enter more deeply into the mystery of the Cross and to unite his suffering and even his loneliness to the paschal font of new life in grace. Benedictine theologian Stanley Jaki relates the moving story of St. John XXIII discussing with Catholic philosopher Etienne Gilson the trials priests were having with celibacy in the 1960s:

> The Pope's face became gloomy, darkened by a rising inner cloud. Then the Pope added in a violent tone, almost a cry: "For some of them it is a martyrdom. Yes, a sort of martyrdom. It seems to me that sometimes I hear a sort of moan, as if many voices were asking the Church for liberation from the burden. What can I do? Ecclesiastical celibacy is not a dogma. It is not imposed in the Scriptures. How simple it would be: we take up the pen, sign an act, and priests who so desire can marry tomorrow. But this is impossible. Celibacy is a sacrifice which the Church has imposed upon herself—freely, generously and heroically."[30]

---

[30] Jaki, "Man of One Wife or Celibacy," 23.

It is a sacrifice that is a powerful means of generating supernatural life by a man uniquely configured to Christ the Head, the author of new life in the Church.

Priestly Celibacy and Consecrated Virginity

While there is certainly an overlap between the purpose of consecrated virginity and that of priestly celibacy, there are distinctions to be made as well. Consecrated virgins imitate the way of life chosen by Jesus, as they do in the counsels of poverty and obedience, in a more literal way and in order to serve as an eschatological witness to life in the Kingdom, in which the resurrected saints "neither marry nor are given in marriage, but are like angels in heaven" (Matt 22:30; Mark 12:25; Luke 20:35). This witness of consecrated virginity, drawing as it does from the long tradition of the Church, cannot be set aside. However, it may be that an overemphasis on this model of following Christ has partially obscured some others. If following Christ perfectly *necessarily* means following him in a radical embrace of virginity, poverty, and obedience, then it is difficult to avoid the well-meaning but dubious conclusion that while he "who marries and has children is a man," he who does *not* marry, for the love of Jesus, "*is yet more a man* because in this respect he is more like the perfect Man, Jesus of Nazareth."[31] From this it is a short step to the claim that every Christian, if he seeks perfection, must become a consecrated religious: a claim directly contrary to the teaching and thought of the Second Vatican Council.[32]

---

[31] See Bertrand de Margerie, *Christ for the World: The Heart of the Lamb,* trans. Malachy Carroll (Chicago: Franciscan Herald Press, 1973), 332, emphasis added.

[32] See Vatican II Council, Dogmatic Constitution on the Church *Lumen Gentium* (November 21, 1964), § 40.

The celibacy of the diocesan priest is not derived primarily from the logic of the evangelical counsels, since he is celibate not primarily for the sake of his own holiness but rather for the sake of his ministry. Or rather, it contributes to his holiness *because* it first enriches his ministry and helps him become a better supernatural father. Indeed it would be difficult to perceive Christ's own celibacy as directed to his holiness, which was already perfect, or as a sign of detachment from the world he came to save, or simply as an expedient to accommodate his itinerant lifestyle.[33] Christ's celibacy can be fully understood only in light of his role in the plan of salvation, his generativity in the order of grace, that is, his fatherhood as the New Adam, Head and Bridegroom of the Church. It is precisely this dimension of Christ's celibacy that gives meaning to the celibacy of the priest as a spiritual father.

Thus, in his celibacy the priest does imitate Christ, but not insofar as Christ is the paragon of humanity. He imitates Christ the Head, to whom he is configured in Holy Orders and whose celibacy was so intimately bound up with his generative role in the salvific plan of the Father. In this, priestly celibacy is distinguished from the virginity of consecrated life.

If consecrated virginity is ordered primarily to eschatological witness, priestly celibacy is ordered primarily to representing Christ in relation to the Church, his Bride, and serving as an instrument of Christ's paternal generativity. If religious virginity is directed primarily to the holiness of

---

[33] See Paul O'Callaghan, "Gli Stati di Vita del Cristiano: Riflessioni su un'Opera di Hans Urs von Balthasar," *Annales Theologici* 21 (2007): 89–90.

the consecrated person, priestly celibacy is directed primarily to the holiness of the Christian people. Both are precious gifts of the Lord to his Church, but they are different gifts and have different aims. The gift of priestly celibacy, imitating as it does Christ's celibacy for the sake of the Church, is a gift ordered primarily to the fulfillment of priestly supernatural fatherhood.

EXERCISING CELIBATE PRIESTLY FATHERHOOD

The priest's celibacy, like his spiritual fatherhood, represents and reveals the paternity of God the Father and does so by reinforcing the threefold *munera* that we examined in the last chapter. This section drills down to the essence of our central question, "Why celibacy?" If celibacy is to be more than merely a symbolic representation of Christ's celibacy, it must have an impact on the lived experience of priests.

Munus Sanctificandi

At a practical level, the sheer availability facilitated by celibacy enables the priest to devote to his sanctifying role the time and energy that otherwise would legitimately be devoted to his family. This consideration, while seemingly mundane, and while not the primary motive for celibacy, is no trifle.

In the life of St. John Vianney, for instance, there is no question that his extensive availability in the confessional, through which he helped reconcile innumerable souls to God, was only possible because of his celibacy. It was not simply the Curé of Ars' availability of time, however, that enabled him to spend so many hours in the confessional but a profound interior and spiritual availability that celibacy made possible. Thus the Second Vatican Council Fathers, in *Presbyterorum Ordinis*, observed that through celibacy priests "more readily cling to him with undivided heart and dedicate themselves more freely in him and through him to the service of God and of men. They are less encumbered in their service of his kingdom and of the task of heavenly regeneration."[34] The interior freedom elicited by the priest's celibacy, in other words, is directly pertinent to his "task of heavenly regeneration," even as St. Paul encouraged some Christians to remain unmarried in order to be "anxious about the affairs of the Lord, how to please the Lord" (1 Cor 7:32). Though his statement is not made in the context of priestly ministry alone, it certainly does apply to celibate priests in a notable way.

The priest's ministry is strengthened by celibacy not just by his physical and interior availability but by a certain moral approachability as well. Contrary, perhaps, to a common impression that celibacy makes a priest less attuned particularly to sexual struggles and marital problems, Karol Wojtyla remarks in *Love and Responsibility* that the priest's lack of direct personal experience of marriage and sexual relations is offset by his pastoral work with so many couples, a wide experience that can be of great benefit to those in his care.[35] An unmarried priest can often apply that pastoral experience more evenly and objectively precisely since it is not colored by his own more subjective experience, and perhaps

---

[34] Vatican II Council, *Presbyterorum Ordinis*, § 16.
[35] Wojtyla, *Love and Responsibility*, trans. H. T. Willetts (New York: Farrar, Straus, Giroux, 1981), 15.

even failures, in marriage.

This moral approachability is most noticeable in the ministry of reconciliation, particularly when it involves sexual matters. Many of the faithful are more, not less, comfortable confessing to a celibate priest. Jean Galot states that it "is undeniable that chastity facilitates the confidence which Christians have in the priest, a confidence which takes on great importance in the accomplishment of the pastoral duty." In his judgment, and in the lived experience of many of us priests, "Christians would enter the confessional less freely if the sacrament entailed the confession of sins to a married priest."[36] To return to the example of the Curé of Ars, Frederick Miller argues that it was the Curé's

> celibacy that drew men and women to him like a magnet and perhaps especially men and women struggling with sexual sins. In a mysterious way, celibacy contributes to the priest's capacity to be the instrument in healing of the wounds of human nature and in the generation of divine life in souls. . . . Many are convinced that the Catholic people confess their sins so freely to their priests precisely because of the grace of celibacy.[37]

Even more importantly, celibacy is eminently suited to the celebration of the Holy Eucharist, identified in the last chapter as the very source of the priest's spiritual paternity. The Eucharist is the sacramental representation of the Pas-

---

[36] Jean Galot, "The Priesthood and Celibacy," *Review for Religious* 24 (1965): 947.
[37] Miller, *The Grace of Ars* (San Francisco: Ignatius Press, 2010), 59.

chal Mystery, the source of all grace and the supersubstantial bread with which the priest feeds his children as well as the liturgical expression of his own paternal headship of the community. In the "sacramental generation" of the Son, the priest images most nearly the eternal generation of the Son by the Father, the prime analogue of all paternity.

Such paternal implications of the Eucharist are complemented by the priest's celibacy. The life-giving sacrificial dimension of the Eucharist finds an echo in the generative, personal sacrifice of celibacy. Behind the Holy Eucharist, said a young Fr. Joseph Ratzinger, "must also always stand the personal sacrificing of the priest who, day after day, gives away his own love, the longing of his life after splendor and happiness, so as to keep himself fully disposed to God."[38] The Holy Sacrifice gives shape and meaning to the priest's own self-oblation and, inasmuch as celibacy is part of that self-gift, it becomes an important component of his paternal generativity. It is most fitting, as others have pointed out, that the man who stands at the altar in the person of Christ and says, "This is my body," refrain from doing so in any other spousal relationship. Thus the Church Fathers often compared priestly celibacy to the ritual continence of priests in the Old Testament.[39] If the priests of the Old Law were to abstain from sexual relations prior to their sacrifice, the Fathers reasoned, all the more should priests of the New Law abstain from sexual relations prior to the Holy Sacrifice of

---

[38] Emery de Gaál, ed., *Homilies at a First Mass: Joseph Ratzinger's Gift to Priests*, trans. David Augustine (Omaha: IPF Publications, 2016), 22. Also see Pope Paul VI, *Sacerdotalis Caelibatus*, §§ 29–30.

[39] See Selin, *Priestly Celibacy: Theological Foundations*, 141–144.

the Mass, of which Temple oblations were only a foretaste.[40]

Celibacy additionally fulfills a symbolic role during Mass in the priest's representation of God the Father. It was observed already that the priest, in a manner of speaking, "generates" the Eucharistic Christ, in effect imaging the Father's generation of the Son. As celibate, he does so more visibly by echoing the "celibate generativity" of the Father in the Son's eternal generation. As celibate, he also echoes the virginal generativity of Mary in the temporal generation of Jesus. Reflecting on the priest's representation of Mary's virginal fruitfulness, the great nineteenth-century German theologian Matthias Scheeben writes that

> the priest conceives the Incarnate Son of God by the power of the same Spirit in order to establish Him in the bosom of the Church under the Eucharistic forms. Thus Christ is born anew through the priesthood by a continuation, as it were, of His miraculous birth from Mary; and the priesthood itself is an imitation and extension of the mysterious maternity that Mary possessed with regard to the God-man. The priesthood is for the Eucharistic Christ what Mary was for the Son of God about to become man.[41]

Munus Docendi

The priest's exercise of the *munus docendi* is also emphasized and strengthened by the practice of celibacy. The previous

[40] See Benedict M. Ashley, *Justice in the Church: Gender and Participation* (Washington, DC: The Catholic University of America Press, 1996), 120–121.

[41] Matthias Joseph Scheeben, *The Mysteries of Christianity*, trans. Cyril Vollert (St. Louis, MO: B. Herder Book Co., 1946), 547.

chapter pointed out that the generativity of the *munus docendi* includes the supernatural fruitfulness of preaching, through which the priest implants the Word of God as a seed that, by the power of grace, blossoms into new life in the souls of his hearers.

Aquinas teaches that celibacy is ordered to contemplation,[42] and it is through contemplation that a priest's preaching is nourished and made supernaturally fruitful. Preaching represents the overflow of the priest's interior life, the "return" that he makes for the privilege of greater intimacy with God. Contemplation is not an isolated, introverted act but fundamentally open to communion, with God and with others. In St. Thomas' memorable image, "even as it is better to enlighten than merely to shine, so is it better to give to others the fruits of one's contemplation than merely to contemplate."[43] Every priest has had the experience of preaching from the fruit of his prayer and the impact that such preaching can have on others. If St. Thomas is right that celibacy can promote a contemplative life, it follows that it can also powerfully contribute to the priest's "fathering with his voice."

Munus Regendi

It is in the *munus regendi*, however, that the priest's celibacy makes the clearest contribution. In parallel to the duties of natural fatherhood, the last chapter examined the role of the spiritual fatherhood of the priest as provider, guide, and protector. Each of these roles is enhanced by the embrace

---

[42] See Aquinas, *Summa Theologiae* II-II, q. 152, a. 2.
[43] Aquinas, *Summa Theologiae* II-II, q. 188, a. 6.

of celibacy. The priest's role as provider includes both the provision of the sacraments for his people, especially the Bread of Life, as well as the provision of other supernatural goods through intercessory prayer. Part of the ordering of celibacy to contemplation just examined, in fact, includes a greater freedom for sustained and intensive intercession for his people, a practice Pope Francis identifies as a stimulus and means of evangelization.[44] Celibacy also frees a man for the active works of charity that make up many of the duties of "natural" fatherhood outlined earlier, and to which a priest's ministry often summons him. To the extent that a priest must fulfill those duties of natural paternity as a component of his spiritual fatherhood, celibacy is therefore ordered to both.

The paternal love of the priest through which he guides and teaches his people in the love of God is also greatly aided by a generous embrace of celibacy. Reflecting on the generosity made possible by celibacy, for example, Pope Pius XII extols the "innumerable army of virgins and apostles who, from the first centuries of the Church up to our own day, have given up marriage to devote themselves more easily and fully to the salvation of their neighbor for the love of Christ, and have thus been enabled to undertake and carry through admirable works of religion and charity."[45]

In recent years, the Magisterium has emphasized this dimension of celibacy that helps the priest respond to the needs of his people. St. Paul VI wrote that celibacy permits

---

[44] Pope Francis, Apostolic Exhortation on the Proclamation of the Gospel in Today's World *Evangelii Gaudium* (November 24, 2013), §§ 281–283.
[45] Pope Pius XII, Encyclical Letter on Consecrated Virginity *Sacra Virginitas* (March 25, 1954), § 26.

the priest "to spend himself wholly for the welfare of all, in a fuller and more concrete way" and it "gives to the priest, even in the practical field, the maximum efficiency and the best disposition of mind, mentally and emotionally, for the continuous exercise of a perfect charity."[46] Pope John Paul II told one gathering of diocesan priests that

> celibacy expresses the profound bond that unites [the priest] to the faithful, those who make up the community born from his [celibate] charism and destined to receive the entire capacity of love that a priest carries inside him. Celibacy, in other words, frees him interiorly and exteriorly, enabling him to organize his life so that his time, his house, his habits, his hospitality, and his financial resources may be conditioned by that which is the scope of his life: the creation around him of an ecclesial community.[47]

The Second Vatican Council sums it up by teaching that celibacy is a "a sign of pastoral charity and an incentive to it as well as being in a special way a source of spiritual fruitfulness in the world."[48]

Such a degree of pastoral charity enjoined upon priests can be difficult. Our culture prizes individual autonomy and

---

[46] Pope Paul VI, *Sacerdotalis Caelibatus*, § 32.

[47] Pope John Paul II, "La Vocazione al Ministero é una Scelta d'Amore: Omelia del Santo Padre Giovanni Paolo II. Santa Messa di Inaugurazione del Convegno 'Spiritualità del Presbitero Diocesano Oggi'," November 4, 1980, author's translation.

[48] Vatican II Council, *Presbyterorum Ordinis*, § 16. Also see Vatican II Council, *Lumen Gentium*, § 42.

personal fulfillment beyond virtually all other goods. Priests live in that same atmosphere and are enticed by those same desires. Celibacy, lived well, can offer a great deal of support to a priest who wishes to exercise generous, self-giving love. A celibate heart is open to all, without preference, as one author states, "to children and young married couples, to the old, to widows, to the sick and the healthy, to the poor and the rich, to sinners and saints."[49] Those who come to the celibate priest seeking pastoral guidance and assistance thus know that they are not his "second" children after his own biological offspring; they know that they, and they alone, come first. Just as a new father finds strength for radical self-giving in his love for his wife and children, so too does a celibate priest find strength for the self-giving demanded by his vocation in the dilation of his heart through the gift of celibacy.

The protective role of a father is likewise enhanced by the priest's celibacy. He protects his spiritual family internally by guarding his flock from error, exhorting and correcting when necessary. To the extent that celibacy detaches the priest from the need for constant personal affirmation from his people, it assists him in fulfilling this dimension of paternity as well.

In a particular way, celibacy prepares the priest to defend the faith against external threats with courage. In the early Church, virginity was a kind of "death to self" that, after the time of the persecutions, symbolically continued the sacrificial witness of the martyrs. In its sacrifice, celibacy fulfills Christ's declaration that "unless a grain of wheat

---

[49] Felices Sánchez, *La Paternidad Espiritual del Sacerdote*, 159, author's translation.

falls into the earth and dies, it remains alone; but if it dies, it bears much fruit" (John 12:24). It is an act of charity, laying down one's life for the sake of supernatural fecundity. Thus, through his celibacy, writes Father (now Bishop) Andrew Cozzens, a priest "is not his own; he has placed his whole life at the service of the mission given him by Christ, which includes not only giving up marriage, but when necessary his possessions and even his own will."[50] Celibacy fortifies him for moral sufferings such as rejection and scorn from a wider secular culture, and it is a stimulus to physical courage, bracing him to endure even death, if necessary, to defend his people and the faith.

One author notes that the Jewish monastic community at Qumran practiced celibacy in order to prepare "for the eschatological Holy War which they believed would usher in the Messianic Age, and they knew that the Law commanded warriors in time of battle to abstain from sex in order to remain in a state of ritual purity and to devote their full energies to battle."[51] In a similar way, celibacy in the New Dispensation frees men "for a fuller dedication to the Holy War"—though it is not a war of bloodshed. It is a "war against the violence and injustice which hold back the Reign of God. They are called not to be the only warriors in this spiritual battle—all Christians are called to that—but the front-line

---

[50] Andrew Cozzens, "*Imago Vivens Iesu Christi Sponsi Ecclesiae*: The Priest as a Living Image of Jesus Christ the Bridegroom of the Church through the Evangelical Counsels" (diss., Pontifical University of Saint Thomas Aquinas, 2008), 336.

[51] Benedict M. Ashley, *Theologies of the Body: Humanist and Christian* (Braintree, MA: The Pope John Center, 1985), 443.

troops who give leadership and courage to the others."[52]

Thus celibacy leaves a priest freer to confront any danger or persecutions that threaten his people, without concern for its consequences to a natural family. In an age that has seen the greatest violations to the dignity of human life in history, both in violent upheavals fueled by tyrannical regimes and in the ongoing and systematic disregard for the dignity of human life by liberal Western democracies, the moment for celibate priests to demonstrate their courageous witness has surely arrived. The purpose of their priestly celibacy, in part, is to free and prepare them for that daunting aspect of their paternal duty, no matter the cost.

THREE PITFALLS OF THE PRIESTHOOD

Beyond the threefold *munera*, reading celibacy in the light of spiritual fatherhood suggests other benefits to the priesthood as well. In particular, it is among the most potent remedies to three broad pitfalls to which I believe we priests are particularly prone today.

Narcissism

Narcissism covers a wide field of human tendencies, but for the purposes of this brief glimpse, it can be characterized as an excessive need for admiration, an extreme sensitivity to criticism, a sense of entitlement, and unreasonable expectations for favorable treatment. Narcissism often includes the craving for creaturely compensations, licit or illicit, which author and theologian Dietrich von Hildebrand identifies as

---

[52] Ashley, *Theologies of the Body*, 443. Also see Eph 6:10–17.

a particular danger of the celibate life.[53] These compensations can include vices such as alcoholism, careerism, pornography, or illicit relationships, or milder alternatives such as an excessive attachment to lavish meals, social events, extensive collections, or exotic vacations.[54] Self-absorption in a priest may also include an obsession with controlling his time, money, and space, such as an inflexible preoccupation with his schedule or protecting his "day off" at all costs. Sometimes it is simply a penchant for creaturely comforts.

Cardinal Joseph Ratzinger, speaking at St. Charles Borromeo seminary in 1990, said that it "is probable that all the great crises in the Church were essentially connected to a decline in the clergy, for whom intercourse with the Holy had ceased to be the fascinating and perilous mystery it is, of coming close to the burning presence of the All-Holy One, and had become instead a comfortable craft by which to secure one's daily needs."[55] Such a bourgeoise approach to the priesthood is often revealed in liturgical aberrations. One of the typical symptoms of narcissism in the priesthood, in fact, pointed out by psychologist Paul Vitz and his priest-son Daniel in a joint article, is a penchant for "personalizing" the Mass, modifying the Church's liturgy to accommodate one's theories or preferences, drawing attention to oneself in order to satisfy a longing for personal affirmation.[56]

---

[53] See Dietrich von Hildebrand, *In Defense of Purity: An Analysis of the Catholic Ideals of Purity and Virginity* (London: Sheed and Ward, 1940), 171.

[54] See John Cihak, "The Blessed Virgin Mary's Role in the Celibate Priest's Spousal and Paternal Love," *Sacrum Ministerium* 15, no. 1 (2009): 151.

[55] Joseph Ratzinger, "Some Perspectives on Priestly Formation Today (Keynote at Symposium on Priestly Formation at St. Charles Borromeo Seminary)," January 20, 1990.

[56] See Paul C. Vitz and Daniel C. Vitz, "Messing with the Mass: The Problem of

A narcissistic tendency particularly prevalent in the priesthood is a "bachelor syndrome," identified by Jesuit author George Aschenbrenner, in which men "become uninvolved spectators. In self-protection, they often radiate a superior, critical attitude and condescendingly carp at people who are seriously involved with the challenges of life."[57] Celibates can be prone to the pride and self-sufficiency in which this sense of superiority is bred. Fr. Raniero Cantalamessa, Preacher of the Papal Household, attributes part of this danger to the celibate's more limited experience with romantic love. "They have never knelt before a creature acknowledging their incompleteness and their need for the other," he writes. "They have never, like a beggar, stretched out their hand to another human being, saying, 'Give yourself to me because I, by myself, am not complete,' which is what a young man says when he declares his love to a young woman."[58]

The aloofness of bachelorhood is sometimes accompanied by a highly administrative or bureaucratic vision of the priesthood, a focus on policies rather than people and their needs, a fixation on liturgical or ceremonial intricacies, or even an obsessive approach to work which may in fact be an attempt to escape the demands of genuine involvement with people. Without the built-in asceticism of marriage, a celibate priest can become detached and uninvolved. As one author writes:

Priestly Narcissism Today," *Homiletic and Pastoral Review* 108, no. 2 (November 2007): 19–21.

[57] George A. Aschenbrenner, *Quickening the Fire in Our Midst* (Chicago: Loyola Press, 2002), 124.

[58] Raniero Cantalamessa, "Dimensions of Priestly Celibacy," in *The Charism of Priestly Celibacy: Biblical, Theological, and Pastoral Reflections*, ed. John C. Cavadini (Notre Dame, IL: Ave Maria Press, 2012), 19–20.

One can be an experienced minister, a competent caregiver, and maintain professional distance. If there is no community life to force the challenge of intimacy, it is just too easy to respond to Christ's call to love one's neighbor by loving humanity 'in general.' Depending on the nature of their friendships, celibates can choose to structure their lives so that there is never any risk of the 'one on one,' never any risk of putting one's own heart on the line. . . . It is not surprising that loving 'in general' seems a safer, saner course. Safe, sane, but potentially sterile.[59]

The "bachelor" priest is not *present*, literally or at least emotionally, to his people and thereby neglects the first responsibility of every father simply to be actively engaged in the life of his family.

It is spiritual fatherhood that liberates a man from these narcissistic manifestations of extended adolescence, in both the natural and supernatural order. A natural father who takes seriously his responsibilities cannot indulge his whims, demand exact control over his life, expect constant personal affirmation, or opt out of his responsibilities at home—and neither can a priestly father. Priestly paternity strikes at the heart of the "bachelor syndrome," which is precisely an abdication of fatherhood and its sense of responsibility for other members of his household.

A strong grasp of supernatural paternity, in contrast, creates a bond of deep intimacy and trust between a priest

[59] Julie A. Collins, "Celibate Love as Contemplation," *Review for Religious* 59, no. 1 (January/February 2000): 81–82.

and his people, a feeling of mutual responsibility, which is the very contrary of self-contented bachelorhood. Galot observes that, while the absence of a wife and natural children might enclose a man on himself, it can also dedicate him to a "deeper and more universal love" if he makes that a conscious decision.[60] In Blessed John Henry Newman's phrase, for celibacy to be "self-transforming" rather than "self-preserving," it must, as in marriage, surrender itself to the other.[61] Through deep friendships and constancy in his pastoral ministry, the priest gains the selflessness that is the ordinary fruit of marriage and family life. He matures in his affectivity, accepts the risk of failure and rejection, overcomes possessive tendencies or complexes that may creep into his heart, and avoids the ever-present pitfall of abstract and generalized, rather than concrete and individualized, love.

Pope Francis adds that the witness of married couples can help draw a man out of himself. Celibacy, he says, "can risk becoming a comfortable single life. . . . In such cases, the witness of married people becomes especially eloquent. Those called to virginity can encounter in some marriages a clear sign of God's generous and steadfast fidelity to his covenant, and this can move them to a more concrete and generous availability to others."[62] The celibate priest, in other words, can resist bachelorhood by allowing himself to fall in love with God and with his people. Pope Benedict XVI

---

[60] Galot, *Theology of the Priesthood*, 246.

[61] See Daniel Cere, "Newman's 'Lesson of the Marriage Ring': Celibacy and Marriage in the Thought of John Henry Newman," *Louvain Studies* 22, no. 1 (1997): 67–68.

[62] Pope Francis, Post-Synodal Apostolic Exhortation on Love in the Family *Amoris Laetitia* (March 19, 2016), § 162.

writes that celibacy "must mean letting oneself be consumed by passion for God and subsequently, thanks to a more intimate way of being with him, to serve men and women, too."[63]

Lived in a fatherly way, supported by a rich and healthy web of relationships, celibacy can become a life so filled with love, so focused on joyful ministry, that it is simply incompatible with the narrow self-absorption of narcissism.

Clericalism

A second danger to the priesthood is that of clericalism: the disordered preoccupation with one's clerical state and status. It is an elitist identification of authority with power rather than humility, with control rather than service, and often includes instrumentalizing others for personal gain or pleasure. Clericalism occurs when a priest places ministry before discipleship, forgetting that he is united to Christ primarily by the baptism that he shares with all believers, not by his ordination.

One of the many consequences of this clericalist mindset is the temptation to convey a veneer of holiness, striving for the appearances of virtue rather than the genuine article in order to cut an appropriately "clerical" figure. At times this deception can promote a subtle, competitive atmosphere between priest and people since a semblance of superiority must be maintained by the priest, particularly when he feels his own inadequacy compared to the people he serves.

Clericalism can also foster a sense of entitlement in which

---

[63] Pope Benedict XVI, "Address of His Holiness Benedict XVI to the Members of the Roman Curia at the Traditional Exchange of Christmas Greetings," December 21, 2006.

priests come to expect an inordinate amount of deference and generosity from those they are called to serve. There can be a haughty demand for obedience and acquiescence from church employees, volunteers, and even parishioners. Temperamental priests give free rein to their mood swings, forcing colleagues and parishioners to put up with their erratic feelings in a way that no good husband and father could. In its most extreme form, this distortion of priestly authority leads to the manipulation of others for emotional or material gain or even for pleasure through sexual abuse.

Once again, it is by embracing genuine priestly paternity that celibate priests can avoid this manipulative exercise of priestly authority. Like Jesus, priests are to give themselves unstintingly to their Bride and generate supernatural children through their instrumental paternity. Jesus explicitly warned his apostles not to "lord it over" others and demanded that his apostles be shepherds, servants—even slaves— and lay down their lives for their sheep (Matt 20:25–28). Authority in the Church is not a matter of domination but of service, not tyranny but covenantal self-gift. "True priestly fatherhood," Dr. Scott Hahn writes, "is the only sure antidote to the recurring ecclesiastical illness called clericalism. We must always remember—you and I—that we are not bosses, not managers, and not administrators. We are fathers."[64]

An openness to authentic friendships with priests and laymen is an important way to avoid the pitfall of clericalism. "It can happen that the seminarian or priest," writes semi-

---

[64] Scott Hahn, "The Paternal Order of Priests," in *Spiritual Fatherhood: Living Christ's Own Revelation of the Father. Third Annual Symposium on the Spirituality and Identity of the Diocesan Priest, March 13–16, 2003*, ed. Edward G. Matthews (Emmitsburg, MD: Mount St. Mary's Seminary, 2003), 5.

nary professor and formator Msgr. Michael Heintz, "under the guise of the celibate commitment, insulates himself from these most basic kind of human relationships and the demands they make, and as a result never really be challenged on a human level." He goes on to say that friends who have a love both for the priesthood and for the priest himself "can challenge, and even cajole, him when necessary, holding him humanly accountable." Heintz insightfully observes that

> the cleric can come to see himself in a kind of exalted position of dispensing or giving to others, a font of grace, but failing to remember that he, too, must be humble enough to receive from others and to reverence others, whether married, single, widowed, or vowed religious, as instruments of grace for the enrichment of his own priesthood. As a result of this kind of solipsism, personal eccentricities or idiosyncrasies can develop unchecked (and these may even work themselves out in a very public way within his celebration of the sacred liturgy), and as his self-awareness decreases or is skewed, his perspective becomes more and more limited, not only in regard to himself but also in regard to others.[65]

In stark contrast to the competitive quality of clericalism, the objective and relational distinction between a father and his child both preserves the truth of priestly authority

---

[65] Michael Heintz, "Configured to Christ: Celibacy and Human Formation," in *The Charism of Priestly Celibacy: Biblical, Theological, and Pastoral Reflections*, ed. John C. Cavadini (Notre Dame, IL: Ave Maria Press, 2012), 75.

and admits of subjective distinctions, including the possible subjective "superiority" of the child. In fact, paternal authority is *affirmed* when the child thrives. All of us who have heard confessions in parishes know that there are some truly holy people sitting in our pews, which is always a source of joy and a holy pride for a confident, paternal priest. A good father pours himself out for his children in love and service, commits all his energy and resources to their growth, and rejoices when they flourish, even—or rather, especially— when they surpass him in excellence.

The very worst manifestation of clericalism, the sexual abuse by clergy, calls for an even more determined return to spiritual fatherhood. It does not even enter the mind of good fathers—frankly, even most bad fathers—to abuse their own children. As one article observes, the

> response of some to the current sexual crisis in the Catholic Church is to say that paternal understandings of authority need to be replaced with functional understandings. As is usually the case with those who dissent from Church teachings, they have it precisely backwards. The most obvious way to ensure fewer instances of clerical abuse in the Catholic Church would be to see that those in charge of seminaries and rectories have a clear understanding of the role of the priest as father. I am not suggesting that this is the only solution to the present crisis, but candidates for the priesthood need to be evaluated for their fitness for fatherhood. A fit father, a

good father, does not abuse his children.[66]

One might add that a good father does not simply recoil at the thought of abusing his children; he also reacts vigorously against anyone who might pose a danger to them. It is not only the sexual abuse by clergy that reveals a flawed notion of priestly authority in recent decades, but the negligent and cowardly response to that abuse by some in authority. Priests and bishops who truly grasp their own paternity will be the most determined and unrelenting in their efforts to protect their supernatural children and to rid the priesthood of those who would use it to exploit others.

Activism

A third common pitfall in the priesthood is an approach to the ministry that loses sight of its supernatural motive and source. It was pointed out earlier that the priesthood is often perceived today as primarily functional and bureaucratic, focused on programs, tasks, administration, and other forms of measurable achievement. It is a vision of the priesthood more in tune with the expectations of the professional workplace than with the demands of the Gospel. St. John Paul II warned that a priest can be tempted "to reduce his ministry to an activism which becomes an end in itself, to the provision of impersonal services, even if these are spiritual or sacred, or to a businesslike function which he carries out for the Church."[67] There are, to be sure, heavy

---

[66] Jennifer Ferrara and Sarah Hinlicky Wilson, "Ordaining Women: Two Views," *First Things* (April 2003): 36.

[67] Pope John Paul II, *Pastores Dabo Vobis*, § 72.

demands—ever more as the number of priests diminishes—placed on the shoulders of those in ministry, and it is unsurprising that even many good priests go through their day frantically working through tasks, often distracted and forgetful of God. The personal availability made possible through cellphones, text messaging, and social media, and the expectation that priests should be reachable almost every minute of the day has further contributed to this restless state of mind. No wonder that many diocesan priests are said to be "overworked and under-prayed."

Refocusing the priesthood on paternity can help overcome this activist mentality. The demands of spiritual fatherhood, like its natural counterpart, cannot be satisfied by moving through a checklist. It is an inherently relational vocation that curbs the tendency of pastoral initiatives to squeeze out the more important moments of interpersonal contact, and supplies an internal standard by which to judge whether those initiatives are truly ordered to the good of souls. Moreover, the very fact that supernatural fatherhood can only be exercised in the order of grace itself counteracts an overly naturalistic approach to its duties. Clericalism and activism, in fact, have this in common: both imagine that one can be a minister of Christ without being a disciple of Christ. The most important work a priest does is not through any achievement or scheme of his own but through the sacraments and through his grace-filled interior life.

Remaining focused on these sources of his paternity will help him retain a contemplative outlook throughout his day and allow him to find God in his ministry and in his people even when his duties seem overwhelming or monotonous. It will give him joy, offer peace in the midst of storms, inspire courage in the presence of obstacles, allow him to see the best in situations and in people, and help him live in the presence of God. "Let no one think that a busy life may not be a holy life," Cardinal Manning wrote. "The busiest life may be full of piety. Holiness consists not in doing uncommon things, but in doing all common things with an uncommon fervour. No life was ever more full of work and of its interruptions than the life of our Lord and His Apostles."[68] In short, a conscious embrace of spiritual fatherhood will help the priest become a man of action with a soul of prayer, generously answering the clamor of his many duties without yielding to the temptation of activism.

At one point in the Gospels, Jesus takes his disciples away for a period of rest—rest that perhaps he wanted as well—but upon stepping out of the boat, they saw crowds waiting for them, looking harassed and helpless, "like sheep without a shepherd" (Mark 6:34). Without another word, without hesitation, Jesus begins to heal and teach and comfort. This is the heart of the master, the generous heart of a father. Some might see the priesthood as a license for detached narcissism, haughty clericalism, or feverish activism. When placed in the light of fatherhood, however, it is precisely the opposite, radically opposed to every form of self-indulgence, self-pity, entitlement, abuse of others, and superficiality. Taken seriously, celibate priestly fatherhood is a path to genuine clerical renewal and reform today, ensuring that the priesthood ever more clearly radiates the humble, joyful vocation of service exemplified in the life of

---

[68] Henry Edward Manning, *The Eternal Priesthood* (Baltimore: John Murphy and Co., 1883), 81.

Jesus the High Priest.

Optional Celibacy?

Celibacy, then, contributes to the priest's own ministry, to his fruitfulness in the order of grace, and to his spiritual fatherhood. Nevertheless, some have understandably asked why celibacy cannot at least be optional, especially given the shortage of vocations and the profoundly disturbing violations of celibacy in recent years. Celibacy is clearly not a prerequisite for priesthood since there are validly ordained priests who are married in the Eastern Churches and by exception in the Latin Rite. It seems like a prudent, even self-evident, choice to make celibacy optional. There is today, as a consequence, tremendous pressure being exerted on the Church to diminish her adherence to celibacy.

Moving toward optional celibacy, however, despite its apparent benefits, would be a great mistake—and for many reasons.

As a path to avoiding sexual abuse, making celibacy optional would miss the mark. Celibacy itself is not the cause of abuse. If it were, then the answer would not be optional celibacy but mandatory marriage! As observed earlier, sexual abuse is no more caused by being celibate than adultery is caused by being married. Allowing priests to marry would not prevent sexual transgressions. Marriage, after all, is regrettably no stranger to scandal. Indeed, the notion that "marrying off" priests will resolve the sex abuse crisis suggests a rather dim view of marriage as well as a certain naiveté about the rate of sexual abuse committed by individuals who are married.

The holy vocation to matrimony is not a cure for sexual drives that are imagined, erroneously, by the popular mind to be irrepressible. The problem is not with celibacy lived; it is with celibacy *badly* lived. The problem is not that wayward priests were unmarried; the problem is that they were unfaithful. Medieval doctors, with the best of intentions, often treated diseases by draining the blood of their patients, unwittingly depriving them of the very nutrients that they needed to get well. Even so, those looking to cure the disease of sexual abuse in the Church by draining her of the grace of celibacy would do little to cure the disease, and yet would deprive the Body of Christ of spiritual nutrients needed to return to health. If we wish to address the problem of clergy sexual abuse, we should begin by expecting the same fidelity from our priests that we expect from everyone else and call them to embrace, through the gift of celibacy, the blessings of priestly fatherhood that we need today more than ever. Otherwise we risk losing all the graces and benefits of celibacy without actually solving the problem of clergy sexual abuse.

Neither is optional celibacy an expedient to relieve a shortage of priests. While there might be a brief surge of new seminarians, the experience of non-Catholic communities that have relaxed their own ordination requirements by no means promises that the surge—if it comes at all—will last. In fact, the push for optional celibacy fails to grasp the cultural landscape in which we live. If marriage is an option, then the blunt reality is that priests who opt for celibacy will be presumed, in the minds of many, to have ambiguous sexual attractions. Moreover, since episcopal ordination would presumably still be limited to celibate priests, as in the Eastern Church, the choice to forgo marriage (and hence remain eligible for the episcopate) would also likely invite cynical conjectures. Optional celibacy would lead to a two-tiered priesthood in which either mediocrity or clerical ambition thrive all too easily.

Even if these pitfalls could somehow be avoided, optional celibacy would throw needless confusion in the path of those discerning the priesthood. Celibacy is a beautiful gift to the Church and to the priest himself, but without a doubt it is sometimes a gift difficult to understand, difficult to receive, and difficult to live—especially for the young. It enkindles a noble generosity in the heart of a young man, but like all deep human loves, the capacity for celibacy takes time to mature. It is true that some seminarians would still choose celibacy, even were it optional. However, who could doubt that many—who otherwise could receive the beautiful grace of celibacy—would simply assume it is not for them? How many graces of celibacy would be forfeited by making it unnecessarily difficult for those in priestly discernment to receive this gift?

There is yet another, even greater difficulty with calls for optional celibacy. The priesthood is not a position over which the Catholic Church has complete control, since it is fundamentally not her priesthood but that of Jesus. Certainly, since there are valid and married priests, it is clear that celibacy is not necessary to exercise the ministerial priesthood. Nonetheless, it is also true that the priesthood itself, which is the priesthood of Christ—that in which all ministerial priests share—is essentially a celibate priesthood. Jesus exercised his ministry on earth as a celibate priest and continues to do so from heaven. Even the Eastern Church, as already noted, limits the episcopate to celibate priests, a sign that celibacy is integral to the priesthood.[69]

This "essential but not necessary" quality of celibacy may be explained by a deep harmony between celibacy and the priesthood. Galot calls this "an essential bond since celibacy conforms to the very nature of the priesthood," though he emphasizes that it "is absolutely necessary neither for the validity of the priesthood nor for the valid and fruitful accomplishment of priestly functions."[70] Celibacy is no more "necessary" to the priesthood, French theologian Bertrand de Margerie writes, than "the Incarnation demanded, in an absolute way, celibacy in the sacred humanity of Jesus."[71] Though not necessary, then, it is eminently suitable, even normative, to the priesthood since, de Margerie continues, it "reflects the very structure of the mystery of Christ and of the Church, which structure it has as its purpose to validate."[72]

Moreover, if supernatural fatherhood is indeed constitutive of the priesthood, and celibacy is ordered to reflecting and exercising that fatherhood, it follows that celibacy is more than an arbitrary "discipline" imposed by ecclesiastical authority. It is only partly subject to the Church's prudential judgment. That is why priestly celibacy (or perpetual continence) has been a part of her life since apostolic times. There has been historical development, of course, but despite repeated calls through the centuries to abandon celibacy, the Church has steadfastly refused to do so. In fact, she has repeatedly reaffirmed the blessing of priestly celibacy

---

[69] See Selin, *Priestly Celibacy: Theological Foundations*, 116–120, 181–182.

[70] Galot, "The Priesthood and Celibacy," 950.

[71] Margerie, *Christ for the World*, 324.

[72] Margerie, *Christ for the World*, 324.

FR. CARTER GRIFFIN

and recommitted herself to fostering it more faithfully in her clergy.

The congruence of celibacy and priesthood, then, is not simply derived from utilitarian considerations arising, for instance, from the difficulty of fulfilling the demands of both a biological and parish family. Rather its normativity is theological since it "belongs to the logic of priestly consecration," in the words of Pope John Paul II, by its suitability and appropriateness.[73] Celibacy is not a "second vocation" that one might or might not have, a mystical gift that hopefully coincides with a priestly call. It flows from the heart of the priesthood as its most fitting accompaniment, a part of the priestly vocation that "is not divisible," Hans Urs von Balthasar says, "to include or not include the charism of virginity; it is always addressed to the whole man, flesh and blood."[74] Theologian Thomas Weinandy even sees in more recent centuries an ever-growing theological conviction in the development of doctrine not toward married clergy but toward the normativity of priestly celibacy:

> Celibacy is intrinsic to the male priestly witness as a "begetter" after the manner of Christ, and, as such, it is much more than a mere canonical law. . . . Instead of seeing a development of doctrine in the normative sanctioning of a married priesthood within the Roman Catholic Church, I would argue that authentic doctrinal development, which is presently groan-

[73] Pope John Paul II, "The Church is Committed to Priestly Celibacy, General Audience," July 17, 1993.
[74] Hans Urs von Balthasar, "The Meaning of Celibacy," *Communio: International Catholic Review* 3, no. 4 (Winter 1976): 324–325.

ing to mature, will confirm that priests, by the very nature of their priesthood, ought normatively to be celibate, for only then is that priesthood exercised in its most complete fashion and to its fullest extent.[75]

The burden of proof, it would seem, rests on those who would challenge the Church's longstanding faithfulness to priestly celibacy. There is not only a historical continuity that would be broken by relinquishing the gift; there is also a profound theological and pastoral congruence with the priestly vocation that would be set aside, at least in part, with manifold repercussions for the salvific ministry of the Church. Proposals to diminish our commitment to celibacy derive, I believe, largely from a spirit of fear and a failure to see the radical claims of the priesthood, rather than from an evangelical spirit of confidence in God's grace. As in every age, God will remain faithful and will enable his priests to live their celibacy well.

Like Christ, the priest is enabled through celibacy to live his own supernatural fatherhood with greater efficacy and naturalness. Celibacy finds its deepest logic not in the order of pragmatism but in the order of love. It is a form of human and indeed sexual fulfillment in which the priest is able to give himself generously, fully, and fruitfully to the Lord and to his people in a powerful way. Abolishing or limiting the gift of celibacy or making it optional, while theoretically possible, would forfeit one of the great gifts to the Church and render more challenging the fullest realization of priestly

---

[75] Thomas Gerard Weinandy, "Of Men and Angels," *Nova et Vetera* 3, no. 2 (2005): 303.

paternity. The pervasive clerical abuse of minors and vulnerable adults represents the by-product of a decadent priestly lifestyle and a rejection of the very priestly fatherhood that would restore and purify the clergy. It is in taking that celibate priestly paternity seriously, forming seminarians and re-forming the clergy in light of the divine call to spiritual fatherhood, where the path to true reform lies.

Chapter Three

Selection and Formation

IT HAS BEEN MY PRIVILEGE for several years to help select
and form men for the priesthood, and I am convinced that
the principles outlined in the previous two chapters yield
very practical applications in this work. If the celibate
priesthood is an essentially paternal vocation, there are
important lessons for the way that priests are chosen and
formed. Without presuming to offer a complete picture of
the qualities that seminarians should have or that seminaries should inculcate, this chapter will attempt to draw some
lessons for those engaged in the work of fostering priestly
vocations and seminary formation.

SELECTING FUTURE SPIRITUAL FATHERS

Masculine Identity

Admitting men to the seminary means preparing them for a
life dedicated to supernatural paternity. It follows that they
must be capable of assuming the mantle of fatherhood, beginning with a desire for the natural paternity that serves as

its model and foundation.

In the mind of Pope Francis, celibacy is so closely aligned to fatherhood that the two cannot be separated in a healthy life. When a man does not have the desire for fatherhood, he said, "something is missing in this man. Something is wrong. All of us, to exist, to become complete, in order to be mature, we need to feel the joy of fatherhood: even those of us who are celibate."[1] Archbishop Vigneron points out that the "human qualities required for a man to succeed as a celibate priest are analogous, if not even identical to those needed for success as a husband and a father. If the man cannot be a good husband and a father, he cannot be a good priest."[2]

The virtues of natural and spiritual fatherhood include, among others, a capacity for sacrificial self-giving, personal responsibility, making and keeping commitments, sincerity, and humility, as well as warmth and tenderness combined with fortitude and seriousness. While all these qualities may not be fully present in every candidate for the seminary, they should be present at least incipiently and their growth should be a priority in seminary formation. Even before these explicit virtues, however, a key criterion in judging the capacity for fatherhood is the stable and confident masculine identity needed to live fatherhood well. Speaking to priests in Warsaw, Pope Benedict XVI reminded them that "Christ needs priests who are mature, virile, capable of cul-

---

[1] Pope Francis, "Morning Meditation in the Chapel of the *Domus Sanctae Marthae*: The Joy of Fatherhood," June 26, 2013.

[2] Vigneron, "Christ's Virginal Heart and His Priestly Charity," *Chaste celibacy: living Christ's own spousal love: Sixth Annual Symposium on the Spirituality and Identity of the Diocesan Priest, March 15–18, 2007* (Omaha, NE: The Institute for Priestly Formation, 2007).

tivating an authentic spiritual paternity."[3] Celibacy only heightens the demand for a confident masculinity.

As is hopefully clear by now, celibacy is not an unearthly, angelic, or "spiritualized" way of living a human life, allegedly compatible with androgynous or effeminate behavior. Rather, celibacy is ordered to fatherhood, which in turn is ordered to fulfilling a man's flesh-and-blood existence as a man. Hence all of the priest's "maleness, his sexuality, his sexual psychology, is a part of his conformation to Christ," as one article observes.[4] Archbishop Fulton Sheen once wrote that the "Church will not ordain a man to his priesthood who has not his vital powers. She wants men who have something to tame."[5] If a man is uncertain of his own masculinity, uncomfortable in his own manhood, or experiences any gender ambiguity or confusion, then it will not be possible for him to reflect the deep, masculine love of Christ for his people. "God calls real men and if there are no men," the Congregation for Catholic Education simply states, "there can be no call."[6]

One crucial indicator of this masculine identity is the ability to interact well and normally with others. While a priestly formation program can attempt to develop this aspect of affective maturity, a certain facility in interper-

---

[3] Pope Benedict XVI, "Address by His Holiness Pope Benedict XVI to the Clergy, Warsaw Cathedral," May 25, 2006.

[4] Guy Mansini and Lawrence J. Welch, "In Conformity to Christ," *First Things* 162 (April 2006): 15.

[5] Fulton Sheen, *The World's First Love* (1952; repr., San Francisco: Ignatius Press, 2011), 96.

[6] Congregation for Catholic Education, "Formation in Celibacy," *Origins* 4, no. 5 (June 27, 1974): 71–72, no. 19. Also see Vatican II Council, Decree on Priestly Training *Optatam Totius* (October 28, 1965), § 11.

sonal relations must first be presumed in candidates for the priesthood before they enter seminary, particularly in candidates who are well past the adolescent years during which social awkwardness is more understandable. Those who are uncomfortable in their own skin, lack conversational skills, have trouble interacting easily with women (and with men), or who struggle to maintain deep and healthy male friendships are not generally going to thrive in the priesthood.

The Question of Same-Sex Attraction

One sign that a priestly candidate does not possess the level of affective maturity demanded by celibate fatherhood is, as the Church has repeatedly affirmed, the presence of deep-seated homosexual tendencies.[7] These tendencies include any evidence of adult homosexual behavior, any advocacy of the so-called "gay culture," or any resistance to the teaching of the Church regarding homosexual inclinations or activity. Same-sex attractions that are deep-seated—that is, not merely superficial or transitory—involve persistent sexual or romantic attractions to persons of the same sex. They also include any aversion to marriage, since the spiritual fatherhood of priests presumes an explicit and heartfelt

---

[7] Most recently in Congregation for the Clergy, *The Gift of the Priestly Vocation: Ratio Fundamentalis Institutionis Sacerdotalis* (Vatican City: December 8, 2016), no. 199–200. Most thoroughly in Congregation for Catholic Education, *Instruction Concerning the Criteria for the Discernment of Vocations with Regard to Persons with Homosexual Tendencies in View of their Admission to the Seminary and to Holy Orders* (London: Catholic Truth Society, 2005), no. 2. For a summary of the consistent position of the Church regarding priestly candidates with same-sex attraction, see Earl Fernandes, "Seminary Formation and Homosexuality: Changing Sexual Morality and the Church's Response," *The Linacre Quarterly* 78, no. 3 (August 2011).

attraction to natural marriage and fatherhood.

This is a difficult matter, and I realize how painful the topic is to good men who struggle with homosexuality. However, there are many reasons why those who experience same-sex attractions should not become priests. The attractions themselves, of course, are not sinful when they are not volitional, and many with a homosexual inclination generously and even heroically resist its temptations. Indeed, it is generally not chosen by those who experience it and may be the tragic result of traumatic experiences in childhood or adolescence.[8] Whatever its "psychological genesis" (a phrase used in CCC 2357), the "objectively disordered" inclinations of same-sex attractions (CCC 2358) reveal an affective immaturity that is an obstacle to the paternity, including priestly paternity, to which masculine human nature is ordered.[9] The greater emotional vulnerability of a man with same-sex attraction is not well suited to the rigors of pastoral ministry, particularly in these times of widespread confusion regarding human sexuality and gender. It is not simply the same-sex attractions, in other words, that render a man unsuitable for priesthood, but the underlying emotional insecurity of which those attractions are a symptom.

This crucial point is missed by those who understand "deep-seated homosexual tendencies" to be simply the

---

[8] For a contemporary review of the data regarding the origins and developmental stages of same-sex attraction, see Timothy G. Lock, "Same-Sex Attractions as a Symptom of a Broken Heart: Psychological Science Deepens Respect, Compassion, and Sensitivity," in *Living the Truth in Love: Pastoral Approaches to Same-Sex Attraction*, ed. Janet E. Smith and Paul Check (San Francisco: Ignatius Press, 2015), 244–278.

[9] See Mansini and Welch, "In Conformity to Christ," 15.

prominence that a candidate gives same-sex inclinations in his personal life. Some, irresponsibly, go so far as to say that homosexual attractions themselves can be a blessing for the priesthood. For instance, Former Master of the Dominican Order Timothy Radcliffe claims that homosexual priests, precisely in their homosexuality, offer unique contributions to the Church. He writes that "we may presume that God will continue to call both homosexuals and heterosexuals to the priesthood because the Church needs the gifts of both."[10] Therefore, in interpreting a 2005 Instruction from the Congregation for Catholic Education about candidates with deep-seated same-sex attractions, Radcliffe argues that such an individual is one "whose sexual orientation is so central to his self-perception as to be obsessive, dominating his imagination. This would indeed pose questions as to whether he would be able to live happily as a celibate priest." But then, he concludes, "any heterosexual who was so focused on his sexuality would have problems too. What matters is sexual maturity rather than orientation."[11] To be sure, a heterosexual man who is obsessed with his own sexual identity and imagination does lack maturity and should not be admitted to Holy Orders either; but it is not sexual obsession alone that rules out the admission of those with same-sex attraction. It is the affective immaturity, the masculine insecurity and ambiguity itself, that the attraction signifies and which renders such candidates unsuitable for priestly fatherhood.

Moreover, where there is no attraction to marriage, there is no sacrificial renunciation, which is one of the es-

---

[10] Timothy Radcliffe, "Can Gays Be Priests?" *The Tablet* (November 26, 2005): 4.
[11] Radcliffe, "Can Gays Be Priests?" 4.

sential graces of apostolic celibacy. Certainly the struggle to live continence itself entails a sacrifice, but as seminary rector Msgr. Andrew Baker points out, "The struggle to live chastely may be extremely difficult for someone with homosexual tendencies, and these struggles would truly be meritorious and virtuous as acts of chastity, but not necessarily of celibacy."[12] Continence alone is not equivalent to priestly celibacy, since it does not necessarily entail the conscious sacrifice of biologically generative sexual union for the sake of a higher generativity.

In fact, it is precisely this lack of a procreative sacrifice that may make celibacy and the priesthood appealing to some homosexual men. The priesthood has at times become a refuge for those fleeing their own sexual attractions, a refuge that bestows a certain legitimacy to their unmarried state. As Pope Benedict XVI said, "Homosexuality is incompatible with the priestly vocation. Otherwise, celibacy itself would lose its meaning as a renunciation. It would be extremely dangerous if celibacy became a sort of pretext for bringing people into the priesthood who don't want to get married anyway."[13] The attractiveness of the celibate priesthood to some of those coping with same-sex attractions obliges the Church to be even more vigilant in screening such candidates from the seminary.

Disciples of Christ with same-sex attractions carry a heavy burden and, with that cross, are called to chastity and sanctity like all other disciples. Nevertheless it is impera-

---

[12] See Andrew Baker, "Ordination and Same Sex Attraction," *America* 187 (September 30, 2002): 9.
[13] Pope Benedict XVI, *Light of the World* (San Francisco: Ignatius Press, 2010), 152.

tive to resist the temptation to admit those with same-sex attraction into the priesthood. While most, if ordained, would likely be able to live sexual continence, the internal struggles of homosexual persons to live chastity are radically amplified, as the startling levels of promiscuity among active homosexual men—even those in committed relationships—suggests.[14] Add to those struggles the spiritual combat faced by priests and the ordinary challenges of celibacy, and it becomes an obligation of justice, not simply obedience to the Church, that demands clarity and steadfastness in the matter. Indeed, in every study of sexual abuse among clergy, the great majority of cases involve the homosexual abuse of boys and young men.[15] However controversial, the wisdom of the Church's resolve has become crystal clear in hindsight. Disregarding it has had shattering consequences in the lives of thousands of young men over the past several decades.

---

[14] For a sampling of statistics on sexual promiscuity among homosexual persons, see https://carm.org/statistics-homosexual-promiscuity. Also see Daniel Mattson, "Why Men Like Me Should Not Be Priests," *First Things* blog, August 17, 2018, https://www.firstthings.com/web-exclusives/2018/08/why-men-like-me-should-not-be-priests.

[15] This is manifest from the 2004 report by the John Jay College of Criminal Justice entitled *The Nature and Scope of the Problem of Sexual Abuse of Minors by Catholic Priests and Deacons in the United States*, commissioned by the U.S. Conference of Catholic Bishops, as well as the August 2018 Grand Jury Report by the Pennsylvania Attorney General. Both of these reports unambiguously show that the majority of sex abuse committed by Catholic priests has targeted pubescent and post-pubescent boys. Fr. Paul Sullins of The Catholic University of America, on behalf of the Ruth Institute, issued a report in November 2018 entitled *Is Catholic clergy sex abuse related to homosexual priests?* which shows a clear causal relationship between homosexuality in the priesthood and the sexual abuse of male minors, debunking the dubious claim of a second John Jay study issued in 2011 that denied any causative relationship between the two.

It is not bigotry or cruelty or "homophobia" that rules out homosexual candidates for the priesthood. It is charity both to the people of God and to the man in question, for whom such a life is manifestly unsuitable and perhaps perilous.

Whatever the consequences of defying the politically correct orthodoxy, we owe it to the faithful, especially to the thousands who have been abused by priests, to take a clear line on the question of priestly candidates with deep-seated same-sex attractions. The emphasis on the paternity of the celibate priesthood helps to confirm the Church's proscription on the ordination of men with same-sex attractions, not because such men are incapable of remaining continent or of achieving great sanctity but because those attractions indicate an ambiguous masculine identity and weaken a man's capacity to exercise celibate paternity fruitfully and joyfully.

FORMING FUTURE SPIRITUAL FATHERS

Anthropologists have observed that fatherhood in general is a cultural effort in a way that motherhood is not.[16] Without the immediacy of the physical and emotional contact that characterizes the relationship of a mother and her child, natural fatherhood relies on a complex and fragile edifice of cultural norms in order to flourish. Apart from its obvious biological component, fatherhood is not so much an inevitable natural reality as a cultural and personal achievement. As we see in the wider community, when this cultural for-

---

[16] Even anthropologists known for more radical views of sexuality and gender, such as Margaret Mead, recognize the important cultural role in father formation. See Margaret Mead, *Male and Female* (Harmondsworth, UK: Penguin Books, 1950), 177–191.

mation is weakened, it does not take long for a culture of paternity to crumble away. The need for formation in fatherhood is no less true for the supernatural paternity of priests. A good seminary will therefore count among its primary aims the formation of strong and confident men, able to assume a celibate commitment and to become faithful fathers in the order of grace.

To some extent, a man learns to be a father by doing the things that a father does. In this respect, much of the formation in priestly paternity will take place in the first years of ordained ministry, as the new priest administers the sacraments, preaches the Gospel, and guides and protects his people. There are, however, many ways that a seminary can help future priests prepare to assume the mantle of spiritual fatherhood. For instance, even presuming adequate screening, suitable candidates for the celibate priesthood may still require formation in their masculine identity. Part of the formation process will therefore include the development of a confident masculinity without any overtones of either effeminacy or "machismo," both of which often reflect sexual and emotional insecurity. It may be that a seminarian's personal experiences of inadequate fatherhood need to be addressed and, as far as possible, healed through healthy paternal examples, clear formation, spiritual direction, and at times anthropologically-sound psychological counseling. This is especially true today when so many young people emerge from broken homes and families, compromised in their ability to understand, appreciate, and exercise generous fatherhood.

Formation for the Munus Sanctificandi
Much of the seminary's formation for spiritual fatherhood

can be centered on the threefold *munera* through which the future priest will exercise his paternity.

Preparing men to exercise the *munus sanctificandi* as a priest is a primary goal of all seminary formation since it is through this office that a priest most powerfully gives supernatural life to his people, above all through the sacraments. It is by a steady growth in holiness that a man becomes more fit to celebrate the sacred mysteries. The validity of sacraments, of course, does not depend upon the holiness of the minister, but his holiness does affect the dispositions of the faithful to receive sacramental graces. While a priest is not necessarily called to a higher degree of sanctity, it can be said that he has a greater responsibility to pursue holiness since the nature of his vocation will likely impact the holiness and salvation of so many.

This obligation to strive seriously for priestly holiness means, first and foremost, that a seminarian must gain a deep appreciation for his own divine sonship. In the natural order, a man is first a son and then a father. He can convey the identity and responsibilities of mature sonship to his own children only when he has lived them himself. This is no less true in supernatural paternity. A priestly father can only pass on the conviction of divine filiation when he is convinced of its significance in his own life first. A seminarian, preparing for a life charged with engendering and forming children of God, will therefore be especially attentive to deepening his own sense of divine sonship by modeling his life on that of the divine Son of God. This is done well in a seminary that has a vibrant, faithful, and beautiful liturgical life and that emphasizes interior growth through personal prayer, Eucharistic piety and adoration, charitable service to others, solid spiritual direction, devotions in common, and spiritual retreats, while fostering a tender devotion to the Blessed Virgin Mary.

Christians "are not ready-made children of God from the start," Pope Benedict XVI wrote, "but we are meant to become so increasingly by growing more and more deeply in communion with Jesus. Our sonship turns out to be identical with following Christ."[17] This is the work of a lifetime. Once, near the end of his life, it is said that Fulton Sheen was asked how long it had taken him to prepare a certain homily. He replied, "About forty years." The same can be said of communion with Jesus, the perfect image of the Father, which is so essential for those who aspire to share in God's own paternity. If this particular call to holiness is true of natural fathers, it is all the more true of the priest whose fatherhood is devoted to fostering that divine communion in the souls of his children.

Formation for the Munus Docendi

Training for the priestly exercise of the *munus docendi* is done in part by forming future priests in the art of preaching and teaching. This will include instruction in skills such as rhetoric, public speaking, and pedagogy. More fundamentally, however, it is again through a consistent life of prayer that a man is prepared to give life through preaching the Gospel. Speaking to priests in Warsaw in 2006, Pope Benedict XVI reminded priests that the "faithful expect only one thing from priests: that they be specialists in promoting the encounter between man and God. The priest is not asked to

[17] Pope Benedict XVI, *Jesus of Nazareth* (New York: Doubleday, 2007), 138.

be an expert in economics, construction or politics. He is expected to be an expert in the spiritual life."[18] It is prayer, the interior life, that overflows into the preaching of a priest who knows the Lord on an intimate basis. The preaching of a holy priest possesses an authority and inner intelligibility— and hence generativity—that can only flow from union with the Lord. There are few requirements of seminary formation that can claim greater urgency than forming seminarians to be men of daily, personal, persevering prayer.

A thorough formation in the Sacred Scriptures and authentic Catholic theology is essential intellectual formation for future preachers. A preacher's efficacy derives from his knowledge and his effort but above all from his intention to preach Christ and the truth of the Gospel, rather than himself. As Pope Benedict XVI emphasized, the function of the priest is to make present "in the confusion and bewilderment of our times, the light of God's Word, the light that is Christ himself in this our world. Therefore the priest does not . . . say his own thing, his own inventions but, in the medley of all the philosophies, the priest teaches in the name of Christ present, he proposes the truth that is Christ himself."[19] When seminarians are formed in an environment of vibrant, confident fidelity to the teachings of the Church, they will inculcate that same fidelity in the souls of those they serve. Indeed, insofar as they begin to teach the faith catechetically, even if only to children, seminarians can already get a glimpse of this paternal generativity that one day

---

[18] Pope Benedict XVI, "Address to the Clergy, Warsaw Cathedral," May 25, 2006.

[19] Pope Benedict XVI, "Christ is Never Absent in the Church, General Audience," April 14, 2010.

they will exercise as priests.

The priest, and hence the seminarian, also exercises the *munus docendi* by teaching through his own good example of faith and virtue. Naturally this is not simply a question of appearing to be holy for the sake of setting a good example but actually being holy. As in the case of natural paternity, theologian Fr. Peter Ryan writes, the virtuous father "does not try to provide good example in front of the children and then misbehave when they are not around, or when he thinks they will not know about it. He knows that would not work in the long run, and he carefully avoids teaching his children hypocrisy and duplicity. When he does something wrong, he tells them it was wrong, and proves to be a good example of repentance and restitution."[20] As Norwegian novelist Sigrid Undset asserted, "Parents have a duty to live in such a way that children can venerate them."

Just as a natural father's moral authority is only credible when it is reinforced by his good example, so too in the supernatural fatherhood of priests. The Second Vatican Council thus urges priests to become "models of the flock . . . mindful that by their daily conduct and solicitude they display the reality of a truly priestly and pastoral ministry both to believers and unbelievers alike, to Catholics and non-Catholics."[21] If their life is not worth imitating, if they are not striving for a life of holiness, it is not surprising when they generate little

---

[20] Peter Ryan, "Second Response to 'Self-Gift in Generative Love,'" in *Spiritual Fatherhood: Living Christ's Own Revelation of the Father. Third Annual Symposium on the Spirituality and Identity of the Diocesan Priest, March 13–16, 2003*, ed. Edward G. Matthews (Emmitsburg, MD: Mount St. Mary's Seminary, 2003), 30.

[21] Vatican II Council, Dogmatic Constitution on the Church *Lumen Gentium* (November 21, 1964), § 28.

fruit. Fostering this authentic holiness, natural and genuine and without pretensions, is an overarching goal of every good seminary formation program.

Formation for the Munus Regendi

Preparing for the *munus regendi* means training seminarians to provide for, guide, and protect the people who will one day be entrusted to their care. Thus, in his love for the Holy Eucharist, the seminarian hungers to provide the Bread of Life to the children of God. In his growth in prayer, he prepares to provide for his people as their priestly intercessor and by preaching from the overflow of his interior life. In shouldering the challenges of seminary life and apostolic assignments, and in his personal experience of God's mercy, he becomes a witness of God's love to others. In the liberating joy of following God without the burdens of undue human respect, he learns to guide his people along the pathways of love in a way that does not generate false and disordered dependencies. In growing in personal confidence, in courage, and in an unwavering desire to promote the good of his people, he learns to exercise the protective dimension of the *munus regendi.* He will become capable of conveying difficult or unwelcome truths in a way that conveys his genuine desire for the well-being of his flock. His leadership will be clear and strong, sometimes challenging, and always considerate and engaging. Preparing in this way to protect his flock from internal disorder and error, the future priest will also develop the courage to confront other external threats which may, from time to time, face the people to whom he is entrusted.

Essential for a priest to exercise the *munus regendi* is a

healthy and well-adjusted regard for divine and ecclesial authority. Fostering a mature approach to those in leadership is therefore an important goal of any seminary culture. One former seminary rector warns of an "Oedipal triangle" that afflicts some priests who perceive the bishop as a domineering father, the Church as a controlling mother, and other priests as competitive brothers. As a result, he says, many reduce their priesthood to a desperate search for affirmation from all three.[22] The point is made somewhat melodramatically, but there is truth in it. Much of the cowardice among priests and bishops that led to the culture of secrecy, cover-ups, and self-protection at the expense of sexual abuse victims can be traced to this sulking and fearful relationship to ecclesial authority. Mature men, by contrast, consciously, freely, and gladly respect the legitimate bounds of proper authority without cringing fear or brooding resentment. They see sound authority and healthy obedience as liberating and as sources of growth. They do not see authority figures as infallible or omnipotent and they feel free to offer suggestions and even correction to them when needed.

In order to help seminarians acquire the virtue of obedience that is upright and manly, docile to legitimate authority and yet courageous enough to challenge authority when necessary, seminary personnel should strive to form an environment that emphasizes growth in freedom rather than merely fearful compliance. Formators should be confident enough in their own paternal authority to model such an environment and to help seminarians develop a confident

---

[22] See Donald B. Cozzens, *The Changing Face of the Priesthood: A Reflection on the Priest's Crisis of Soul* (Collegeville, MN: The Liturgical Press, 2000), 54–60.

leadership style for the future exercise of their own priestly authority.

Even with the best of environments, however, the suspicion of authority so endemic in our culture may, regrettably, be too deeply rooted in some candidates to be overcome in seminary formation. Since their exercise of obedience will always be a struggle, these candidates should not be advanced in formation.

Fathers Forming Fathers

By consistently casting and recasting the priestly vocation in the light of paternity, seminary formators will ensure that it does not remain a disembodied concept but rather evokes concrete acts of generosity and a wholehearted determination by the seminarian to embrace his own development as a future father. Those charged with the ministry of priestly formation are responsible for nurturing such a culture. It follows that priests chosen for seminary work must themselves be capable of giving a practical, authentic, lived witness of mature masculinity and celibate priestly fatherhood. This witness will help seminarians assume supernatural paternity not only through formal means of formation but, perhaps even more effectively, by the seminary fathers exercising their own spiritual paternity with the seminarians themselves. It is always in receiving the gift of paternity that men are best made ready to exercise it.

It is not just the witness of spiritual fathers, however, that a seminarian—indeed every priest—needs. The wisdom and the witness of biological fathers can also contribute to the formation of priestly paternity. Their experience of paternity, often in the crucible of suffering and generous self-gift, can affirm priests and seminarians in the nobility of their vocation, offer irreplaceable lived experience, and remind them that sacrifice is always united to the joys of paternity. "What good parents are capable of doing for their biological children," notes Raniero Cantalamessa, "the level of self-forgetfulness that they are capable of attaining to provide for their children's well-being, their studies, and their happiness—must be the measure of what we should do for our spiritual children and for the poor."[23] As Notre Dame Professor John Cavadini asks, isn't there a way that he, as an experienced father, can guide a newly ordained priest

> so that he can little by little understand what it means to be a "Dad"—and slowly grow into that role, in the way suited for his state in life? And, can't I learn, too, about the essence of my own fatherhood from someone like Bishop D'Arcy, who was never married and has no kids but somehow in the lifelong exercise of pastoral charity had shown me a spiritual fatherhood that I recognize as real fatherhood partly by the way it catches up my own version into something "higher" not by negation but by affirmation? . . . Without the witness of those whose fatherhood is solely spiritual, natural fatherhood can collapse in on itself and become chauvinism. Without the example, living and effective and authoritative, of literal fathers, spiritual fatherhood becomes gnosticized.[24]

[23] Cantalamessa, "Dimensions of Priestly Celibacy," in *The Charism of Priestly Celibacy: Biblical, Theological, and Pastoral Reflections*, ed. John C. Cavadini (Notre Dame, IL: Ave Maria Press, 2012), 24.

[24] Private correspondence with the author on February 18, 2012.

Natural fathers and priests can thus be of great support to each other. The similarity between their "mutual life of sacrifice is perfect for extending to one another mutual affective and spiritual support. Ideally," theologians Perry Cahall and Deacon James Keating add, "the dads of the parish should be the most faithful friends of the priest."[25] All the more can they be great models and mentors to young men preparing for the priesthood as seminarians.

Formation in priestly fatherhood should therefore be intentional and comprehensive throughout the years of seminary. Just as the wider culture has an important role to play in the formation of natural fathers, so too does the seminary culture have an important role to play in the formation of spiritual fathers. Being a seminarian is somewhat like the time of anticipation for a man expecting his first child as he readies himself to take on new responsibilities and a new title. A remarkable change often comes about. His self-absorption gives way to a sense of responsibility and a desire to pour himself out for his wife and child. Fatherhood draws a man out of himself, widens his heart to embrace his new child, and fortifies him for the daily sacrifices needed to support his family. The compelling vision of priesthood lived as a vocation of spiritual paternity has the potential to effect a similar change in the heart of a young man preparing for priestly ministry.

---

[25] Perry J. Cahall and James Keating, "Spiritual Fatherhood," *Homiletic and Pastoral Review* 110, no. 2 (November 2009): 19. See also Pope Francis, Post-Synodal Apostolic Exhortation on Love in the Family *Amoris Laetitia* (March 19, 2016), § 162.

Forming Chaste Fathers

Celibacy is a powerful motive and support for the exercise of priestly fatherhood and a source of tremendous joy and satisfaction for the priest, but it cannot be denied that at times it is a challenging road to travel. Forming men for priestly celibacy means directing their sexual energies in a positive direction, toward generating new life in the order of grace and building up the Kingdom of God. Celibacy cannot remain a debilitating burden for those in Holy Orders, and if a seminarian appears incapable of living celibacy faithfully and joyfully, he should not be advanced to ordination.[26] While insisting that celibacy is manifestly not the cause of sexual infidelity among priests, it is certainly true to say that unchastity *is*. In common with every age, then, celibate men must learn habits that lead to sexual and personal integrity. The hyper-sexualized culture in which most priests will exercise their ministry today makes this dimension of formation more imperative than ever. Fostering good habits in the heart of every seminarian is thus a crucial task for every seminary and formator.

Such formation begins with a vibrant and positive view of human sexuality itself and the capacity to love. As incarnate spirits, every human being is a sexual being, male or female—the one human difference explicitly willed by God at Creation (Gen 1:27). This is as true for the celibate priest as it is for the married layman, and any good formation program will foster a healthy acceptance of the body. "Human sexuality, as we know today," Raniero Cantalamessa writes,

---

[26] See Congregation for the Clergy, *The Gift of the Priestly Vocation*, no. 110.

"is not confined solely to its procreative function but has a vast range of possibilities and resonances within a person, some of which are fully valid for celibates and virgins. The celibate and the virgin have renounced the active exercise of sexuality but not sexuality itself. It is not something we leave behind. It remains and 'informs' so many expressions of a person. The celibate does not cease being a man, nor does the virgin cease being a woman."[27]

This essential goodness of being human is nevertheless accompanied by the passions, which, good in themselves, can also lead us into sinful actions. The sexual urge is especially powerful and hence requires special attention and discipline. It is the virtue of chastity that enables a person, whatever his vocation, to temper and channel his sexual desires in a positive and life-giving way. Chastity guards our capacity to love, protecting it from the shackles of sin that would eventually devour us. C. S. Lewis wisely observes that sometimes we "give our human loves the unconditional allegiance which we owe only to God. Then they become gods: then they become demons. Then they will destroy us, and also destroy themselves. For natural loves that are allowed to become gods do not remain loves. They are still called so, but can become in fact complicated forms of hatred."[28]

Chastity, then, is a freedom *from* sin, but even more importantly it is a freedom *for* authentic friendship and communion. It is a freedom for holy purity. The great Catholic writer and apologist Frank Sheed remarks that "chastity as

---

[27] Cantalamessa, "Dimensions of Priestly Celibacy," 20–21.
[28] C. S. Lewis, *The Four Loves* (San Diego: Harcourt Brace Jovanovich, 1960), 19–20.

such is merely a fact of one's autobiography. It means that one has not had a particular bodily experience. If this is for the love of God it is a virtue; but not if it is only because one is afraid of women, or has no natural inclination to women, or prefers one's stamp collection. But purity means the direction of energy to God with no admixture of self."[29] True chastity (what Sheed calls purity) puts order into human loves, whatever one's vocation, and allows us to interact naturally and in healthy ways with both men and women. It is not the most important virtue—that would be charity—but it is indispensable to the life of holiness.[30] One simply cannot make progress in the spiritual life, let alone the priestly life, without it.

Even as learning the rules of painting or sheet-music enables one to produce beautiful paintings and harmonious music, so too do the rules of chastity harness the power to love in a way that is truly enriching. When these rules are inculcated at an early age and fostered in the family in a clear, healthy, and positive way, it is far easier for a young person to preserve a well-integrated chastity through the tumultuous years of adolescence. Regrettably, this often does not happen. Many parents do not understand their role in fostering chastity in their children—if they accept the need for chastity at all—and seemingly the entire cultural apparatus of social media, internet videos, music, video games, movies, and television shows all seem to be working in concert to loosen the grip of young people on this crucial virtue.

---

[29] Frank Sheed, *Theology and Sanity* (San Francisco: Ignatius Press, 1993), 460–461.
[30] See Congregation for the Clergy, *Directory for the Life and Ministry of Priests*, no. 82.

Seminarians are not immune from these wider cultural influences. Many come to the seminary with sexual experiences of their own, including exposure to internet pornography—often at a very tender age when it can cause the most confusion and plant the most stubborn seeds of future sexual addictions.

Though we must sympathize deeply with the injustice that has been done to them by this toxic fallout of the sexual revolution, it is nevertheless important for every seminarian to understand, in no uncertain terms, the expectation that he develop comprehensive and authentic chastity prior to ordination. An environment of transparency and open sincerity in the seminary—in both the internal forum of spiritual direction and the external forum of formation advising—is essential so that seminarians are comfortable speaking plainly about the struggles, aspirations, and desires that they experience.[31] In this way, though a healthy and mature seminarian does not cease being attracted to women, he can learn to integrate those feelings well, bring them to prayer, speak about them to his spiritual director and other mentors, and find in healthy friendships, apostolic work, and a balanced life positive outlets for his capacity to love.

As he makes his way toward a definitive embrace of celibacy, there should be clear parameters along the way. Sexual activity, of whatever sort, with any other person, constitutes grounds for dismissal from the seminary. Any use of internet pornography should be relentlessly tackled, using all available natural and supernatural means, until the habit is

---

[31] See Pope Paul VI, Encyclical Letter on the Celibacy of the Priest *Sacerdotalis Caelibatus* (June 24, 1967), §§ 67–68.

broken. Chronic and serious struggles to remain chaste in thought, word, or deed become progressively more concerning, and ultimately disqualifying, as a man moves closer to ordination. "It would be gravely imprudent to admit to the sacrament of Orders a seminarian who does not enjoy free and serene affective maturity," the 2016 *Ratio Fundamentalis Institutionis Sacerdotalis* states. "He must be faithful to celibate chastity through the exercise of human and priestly virtues, understood as openness to the action of grace, rather than the mere achievement of continence by willpower alone."[32]

To this end, seminarians must be taught all the means necessary to grow in authentic chastity. The Second Vatican Council taught that

> the more that perfect continence is considered by many people to be impossible in the world of today, so much the more humbly and perseveringly in union with the Church ought priests demand the grace of fidelity, which is never denied to those who ask. At the same time they will employ all the helps to fidelity both supernatural and natural, which are available to everybody. Especially they should never neglect to follow the rules of ascetical practice which are approved by the experience of the Church and are as necessary as ever in the modern world.[33]

The natural means to grow in chastity include a healthy dis-

[32] Congregation for the Clergy, *The Gift of the Priestly Vocation*, no. 110.
[33] Vatican II Council, Decree on the Ministry and Life of Priests *Presbyterorum Ordinis* (December 7, 1965), § 16.

trust of self and avoiding the occasions of sin; knowing the signs of vulnerability such as boredom, sadness, loneliness, discouragement, and fatigue; temperance in the use of the internet, mobile devices, and social media; guarding the senses and especially custody of the eyes; setting clear boundaries in friendships with women, similar to those of a responsible married man; a balance of life that includes work, prayer, exercise, and wholesome recreation; regular exposure to beauty in art, literature, and music; and fostering deep and authentic friendships with men, especially brother seminarians. Formation in mature obedience and simplicity of life, with all their practical sacrifices and detachments, will also offer many parallel benefits for growth in chastity.

The supernatural means to grow in chastity include a vibrant interior life, daily mental prayer, frequent confession and daily examination of conscience, an awareness of the spiritual combat, and a trusting confidence in the maternal protection of the Blessed Virgin.[34] Of particular note is the power of Eucharistic Adoration, ideally a daily practice in the seminary, "one of the best antidotes to the hypersensual and hypervisual culture we live in," Michael Heintz argues. "In stark contrast to the glitz and glam, the flash and fury of the images thrown at us by the various media," he writes,

> Christ reveals himself to us in the simplest of forms, in the seemingly most ordinary of elements, in a way that is emblematic of the entire divine economy, stooping down to us to show us himself, to give

[34] For a list of natural and supernatural means to grow in chastity, see Congregation for the Clergy, *Directory for the Life and Ministry of Priests*, no. 82.

himself, and to heal our swelling pride by his own divine humility. In an age when we face sensual sensory overload, to stop, to pause, to fix our gaze on Christ, and to have our imaginations shaped by him who gave himself for us should be a regular feature of seminary formation and of the ongoing formation of every priest.[35]

The self-mastery of chastity will seldom be won apart from a wider pursuit of temperance and self-denial. As a seminarian grows in these moderating habits and resists the spirit of compensation and indulgence, he will find it easier to grow in chastity as well. Self-denial includes small mortifications throughout the day, as well as regular habits of mortification of body, sense, imagination, and memory.[36] An important arena of mortification is in the quest for personal order and discipline, which will give him consistency in spiritual practices, diligence in work, and a balance of life that will be highly conducive to growth in chastity. As the Secretary of the Congregation for Catholic Education wrote when *Pastores Dabo Vobis* was issued:

Chastity is not a gospel flower enclosed within some greenhouse, but growing alongside all the other

---

[35] Michael Heintz, "Configured to Christ: Celibacy and Human Formation," in *The Charism of Priestly Celibacy: Biblical, Theological, and Pastoral Reflections*, ed. John C. Cavadini (Notre Dame, IL: Ave Maria Press, 2012), 81.

[36] See, for instance, Congregation for Catholic Education, "Formation in Celibacy," 73, no. 23. Also, Pope John Paul II, Post-Synodal Apostolic Exhortation on the Formation of Priest in the Circumstances of the Present Day *Pastores Dabo Vobis* (March 15, 1992), § 48.

blooms in the garden of evangelical life. It needs a positive, orderly, clean, outdoor environment; chastity harmonizes with the demands of work and study, grows stronger in the commitment of a genuine personal and community piety, expands in the fellowship of human relations. It needs to be balanced to be healthy, it needs regular times set aside for rest and recreation, the activity of some kind of sport, and some kind of artistic or intellectual hobby; it matures with the initial experiences of apostolate and service to others. The celibate life takes shape and draws strength in the joy of open fellowship, where deeds, words and duties are steeped in truth and cordiality[37]

When he has started to make significant progress toward genuine chastity, the seminarian is in a far better position to discern the call to celibacy and to be formed for it. This is because celibacy is a way of loving sexually—the gift of body and soul to God and to others, ordered to universal charity, to all men and women—and is a privileged way of living supernatural fatherhood. It is a way of loving that is spiritual but also entirely human, a supernatural calling that can only be fully lived through the power of grace embraced by human effort. Love always involves sacrifice and suffering, and chaste celibate love is no exception. Nevertheless, as countless priests have demonstrated, it can be a profound blessing

---

[37] Jose Saraiva Martins, "Training for Priestly Celibacy," accessed October 5, 2018, http://www.vatican.va/roman_curia/congregations/cclergy/documents/rc_con_cclergy_doc_01011993_train_en.html.

to the Church and, for the man himself, a path to personal joy in a life lived for the sake of the Kingdom of God.

Chapter Four

Further Benefits of Celibacy

ABOVE THE ALTAR of the Venerable English College in Rome hangs a painting of the Blessed Trinity by Durante Alberti. The painting holds a privileged place in the heart of every English priest. In the sixteenth century, each time one of the College's graduates had been captured and brutally executed in England, the seminarians gathered before that painting and sang the *Te Deum*, the Church's most cherished hymn of praise, to thank God for the gift of their brother's perseverance and the blessing of a new martyr. The readiness of those young men to embrace almost certain martyrdom after ordination was made possible, in part, by their radical commitment to celibacy. So too was their ardent desire to preach the Gospel in their native land, to teach the faith to the many unformed Catholics, and to offer the sacraments at great personal risk.

These are the responsibilities and blessings of spiritual paternity, so deeply embedded in priestly celibacy, that we have already considered at length in the first three chapters. But there are additional graces of celibacy for the priest himself, for the Church and the people he serves, and for the world at large. They are among the choice gifts that the Lord left to his Church through the gift of priestly celibacy.

Graces of Celibacy

Holiness

Though the celibacy of the diocesan priest is not, as already observed, ordered primarily to his personal holiness, none-theless, by enhancing his ministry it can also thereby contribute to his sanctification. The Second Vatican Council taught that through celibacy priests "cling to [Christ] with an undivided heart and dedicate themselves more freely in him and through him to the service of God and of men. . . . In this way they become better fitted for a broader acceptance of fatherhood in Christ."[1] This "undivided heart" of the celibate priest reflects his renunciation of marriage and natural children for the sake of an even higher good. The Council exhorted all priests who "have of their own free choice accepted consecrated celibacy after the example of Christ, to hold fast to it with courage and enthusiasm, and to persevere faithfully in this state" by praying for the grace of fidelity and fulfilling "the rules of ascetical practice" that are as needful today as ever.[2] The offering of celibacy is therefore ordered to holiness by encouraging a life more fully dedicated to God, inviting the priest to embrace his paternity more generously, and by fostering an ascetical attitude that can be the occasion of growing in grace.

---

[1] Vatican II Council, Decree on the Ministry and Life of Priests *Presbyterorum Ordinis* (December 7, 1965), § 16.

[2] Vatican II Council, *Presbyterorum Ordinis*, § 16.

Fr. John Cihak, author of many insightful articles on the priesthood, notes that there is an asceticism in celibate priesthood that is grounded in the "essential felt loneliness in the Cross," an ache for the consolation of marriage and children with which the celibate must contend.[3] As St. Teresa of Calcutta once observed to priests, "Your priestly celibacy is the terrible emptiness you experience. God cannot fill what is full, he can fill only emptiness. . . . It is not how much we really 'have' to give, but how empty we are—so that we can receive fully in our life and let him live his life in us."[4]

Like nature, the human heart (so to speak) abhors a vacuum, and it will be filled. When celibacy is lived badly, that vacuum is often filled with human acclaim, questionable recreations, the pleasures of the table, gadgets, expensive hobbies or collections, sexual gratification—the list is practically endless. When celibacy is lived well, however, with an interior life and with generosity, that same vacuum will be filled with God and the things of God, the fruitfulness and the inexpressible joys of celibate paternity.

The witness of innumerable priests through the ages demonstrates that God gives his servants every grace and every opportunity they need to live celibacy well. In receiving those gifts, the priest grows in conformity to the One in whose paternity he shares and in his dedication to the ministry. Through these gifts, he grows in personal holiness.

---

[3] Cihak, "The Blessed Virgin Mary's Role in the Celibate Priest's Spousal and Paternal Love," *Sacrum Ministerium* 15, no. 1 (2009): 159.

[4] Teresa of Calcutta, "Priestly Celibacy: A Sign of the Charity of Christ" (1993): accessed October 5, 2018, http://www.vatican.va/roman_curia/congregations/cclergy/documents/rc_con_cclergy_doc_01011993_sign_en.html.

Pastoral Charity

A second spiritual good of celibacy is a stimulus to intensify his pastoral charity for God's people in a life of generous priestly service. As noted in the last chapter, a change occurs in every man's heart when he becomes a biological father. His very identity is transformed. He is forever a "father" with all the responsibility it entails. Looking upon his newborn child, Cahall and Keating write, "a man can feel utterly overwhelmed, and can be struck by the realization that he is now called upon to give himself completely to protect the preciousness that he sees before him."[5] He is invited into a new life of self-giving generosity.

When a child is born, there are two births: the child is born into life and the man is born into fatherhood. Grasping the full significance of his new identity can be a daunting experience for a new father. By responding to the demands of paternity wholeheartedly, a man allows his entire life to be transformed by the daily responsibilities of a family: the sleepless nights, the financial concerns, and the loss of privacy and accustomed recreations. Nevertheless, in his generous response, a father finds the satisfaction for which his heart longs. One father writes that despite the initial shock of paternity,

> through the exhaustion, financial stress, screaming, and general chaos, there enters in at times, mysteriously and unexpectedly, deep contentment and gratitude. . . . Everything he does, from bringing home a

---

[5] Perry J. Cahall and James Keating, "Spiritual Fatherhood," *Homiletic and Pastoral Review* 110, no. 2 (November 2009): 16.

paycheck to painting a bedroom, has a new end and, hence, a greater significance. The joys and sorrows of his children are now his joys and sorrows; the stakes of his life have risen. And if he is faithful to his calling, he might come to find that, against nearly all prior expectations, he never wants to return to the way things used to be.[6]

This experience, both its challenge and its joy, is no less true in spiritual paternity. The supernatural fatherhood of Christ himself followed this pattern of suffering that opens up to the joy of new life. Jesus gave himself to others without calculation and without limit, and in his Incarnation, death, and Resurrection his paternity was born. In surrendering all, Christ emerged triumphant and joyful in the Resurrection and continues to pour out his life of grace for the generation of new life. By sharing in the fatherhood of Christ, the priest also shares in this Paschal Mystery and follows the same path.

St. John Vianney identified the priesthood with "the love of the heart of Jesus."[7] The priest's paternity, like that of Christ and like that of natural fathers, will only come to fruition if he pours himself out generously. The expansion of a man's heart who first gazes upon his newborn child can and should happen in the heart of every priest who grasps his own genuine paternity and the responsibility that it en-

---

[6] Andrew Peach, "On the Demise of Fatherhood." *First Things: On the Square* (June 17, 2009): accessed October 5, 2018, http://www.firstthings.com/onthesquare/2009/6/on-the-demise-of-fatherhood.

[7] St. John Vianney, quoted in B. Nodet, *Jean-Marie Vianney*, Curé d' Ars, 100; cited in CCC 1589.

tails. Like the natural father whose cares and obligations have grown but who finds in his generous response a deeper joy than he ever thought possible, the priest, too, is prompted to make a radical gift of himself on behalf of his people. In making that gift, he will find his deepest satisfaction. In this, as in so many other areas, priests have much to learn from biological fathers. Like them, the priest is not called simply to fulfill certain paternal functions, not simply to serve his people, but to love his people with all his heart. By virtue of his paternity, the priest places at their disposal all the strength and capacity of his masculine nature, and in doing so brings his personality to its maturity and fulfillment.

"One of the graces of celibacy," Archbishop J. Peter Sartain writes, "is that in Christ our family expands to include all those to whom he sends us. No matter their age, race, culture, or language, they are our children—and they have a claim on us."[8] The priest, paradoxically, can only experience freedom by committing himself to others, he can only find himself by losing himself in sacrifice, and he can only receive the gift of joy by giving himself generously to his people.

Fidelity

A third spiritual good of celibacy is a greater motivation to be faithful to the Church and to her teachings. The priest's fatherhood, derived from his configuration to Christ the Head, is mediated through the motherhood of the Church as the Bride of Christ. Just as a man who becomes a father is

[8] J. Peter Sartain, "Beloved Disciples at the Table of the Lord: Celibacy and the Pastoral Ministry of the Priest," in *The Charism of Priestly Celibacy: Biblical, Theological, and Pastoral Reflections*, ed. John C. Cavadini (Notre Dame, IL: Ave Maria Press, 2012), 136.

especially bound to exhibit a refined and constant fidelity to his wife, so too is a priest, conscious of his paternity, moved to an even deeper love for the Church, the mother of his children. He will be especially mindful to demonstrate a visible adherence to her teachings and her guidance, knowing that few things are more detrimental to the unity of a family than one of the parents undermining the authority of the other. In fact, the priest's own generativity is at stake in the measure that he is faithful to the Church, since it is her credibility as their common spiritual mother that enables a priest to preach confidently the faith transmitted by the apostles to their successors. As Archbishop Coakley states, "Our being in mindful and heartfelt communion with the Church is what gives our ministry its power of generativity."[9]

In faithfully transmitting her teachings, the paternal priest radiates an unfeigned love for the Church that is conveyed almost unconsciously to those he serves, somewhat as a man's love for his wife is communicated unconsciously when he speaks of her. Through his fidelity, the priest offers his supernatural children the precious gift of love and admiration for their own mother, one of the greatest gifts that any natural or supernatural father can bestow.

As in marriage, this love for the Church is a matter of choice on the part of the priest, hard work, and sometimes heroic sacrifice. Thus Dr. Scott Hahn confides in seminarians and priests the key to a thriving family:

---

[9] Paul S. Coakley, "The Priest as Father 101," in *Spiritual Fatherhood: Living Christ's Own Revelation of the Father. Third Annual Symposium on the Spirituality and Identity of the Diocesan Priest, March 13–16, 2003*, ed. Edward G. Matthews (Emmitsburg, MD: Mount St. Mary's Seminary, 2003), 38.

The secret is this: strive to fall more in love with your bride every day, and with the children she has given you. By now, you are grown men, and you have probably known many married couples who have "fallen out of love." . . . The analogy applies just as well to the priestly fathers who abandon their bride, the Church, and her children—and to those who stay with her, grudgingly and in misery. Falling in love is usually involuntary. Staying in love, however, demands will and work and help from almighty God. But the rewards are well worth our effort.[10]

Fraternity

A fourth spiritual good of priestly celibacy is a greater motivation to strengthen the fraternal bond among priests.[11] Flowing from his fidelity to the Church and stimulated by the consciousness of his own paternity, a priest is also encouraged to strengthen his union with his brother priests, the fellow-fathers with whom he labors.

Celibacy provides the emotional space and a shared priesthood provides the spiritual space for deep and abiding friendships among priests. In an age with fewer priests, these fraternal bonds are more necessary than ever. Indeed, at a time with fewer male friendships in general, the presbyteral brotherhood provides a witness to other men that

---

[10] Scott Hahn, "The Paternal Order of Priests," in *Spiritual Fatherhood: Living Christ's Own Revelation of the Father. Third Annual Symposium on the Spirituality and Identity of the Diocesan Priest, March 13–16, 2003*, ed. Edward G. Matthews (Emmitsburg, MD: Mount St. Mary's Seminary, 2003), 4–5.

[11] See Pope Paul VI, Encyclical Letter on the Celibacy of the Priest *Sacerdotalis Caelibatus* (June 24, 1967), §§ 79–80.

male friendship is still possible and even constitutive of a fulfilled life. Many priests, for instance, have initiated men's groups in their parishes, fostering the kinds of friendships among laymen that they already enjoy among their brother priests. Most of these groups meet at inconvenient hours—very early on Saturday mornings for instance—to avoid disrupting other family activities. That so many men are willing to do so, that so many are willing to sacrifice for spiritually-sound male friendships, is revealing. The celibate fraternity of priests can provide them encouragement and a lived example today.

Moreover, a key sign of health in a presbyterate is the zeal with which priests enkindle the flames of a priestly vocation in the hearts of young men. Since that zeal for vocations is often the fruit of the fraternity that priests enjoy, a vibrant vocations program is indirectly another spiritual blessing of priestly celibacy. Catholic psychiatrist Conrad Baars comments on the compelling witness of strong and paternal priests:

> I cannot see how young men, whole, *caelebs* [single], virtuous, masculine, and well-educated could fail to respond to the call of the beautiful and virile vocation of the priesthood. I cannot see how they could not be eager to assume the priest's task of bringing men the love of God by being an *alter Christus* [other Christ], by teaching the divine truths without fear of hurting people's feelings or being unpopular, by exposing and opposing heresies, by upholding the law of Christ, by their willingness to risk betrayal, imprisonment, torture, and death in bringing Christ

to the captive nations, by being leaders in the unrelenting battle against moral evil. I cannot see how mature young men could not long to affirm the living Christ in His continued, infinite love of all men by responding to His love in the name of many.[12]

As every successful vocations program will affirm, it is the witness of faithful, generous, virile priests, united in fraternal bonds, that most strongly radiates the attractiveness of the priestly calling.

Priestly Identity

A fifth spiritual good of celibacy, among many that might be chosen, is an affirmation of the priest's identity. It has already been observed that for many, priestly identity has given way to a functionalism that increasingly regards ministry as a series of programs and administrative tasks. The retrieval of the priest's identity means recapturing not *what* but *who* he is. An important part of that identity is to be found in his own celibate priestly fatherhood. Such an identity reminds the priest of his purpose in life, his place in the world, and enables him to convey an identity to his people as children of God.

Becoming fully conscious of his own fatherhood is a transforming moment in the life of a priest, as it is for every man. With its roots in Scripture and Tradition, in the patristic age and the contemporary Magisterium, and in his masculine inclinations and his conformity to Christ the

---

[12] Conrad W. Baars, *A Priest for All Seasons: Masculine and Celibate* (Chicago: Franciscan Herald Press, 1972), 48.

Head, paternity is a role with which the priest can identify and into which he can pour his energies with complete confidence. No man was made less a man by striving to become a better father.

Casting celibacy in the light of authentic human paternity does not, then, "spiritualize away" man's natural inclinations. In fact, by showing that celibacy is a privileged way of living the supernatural fatherhood to which all men—including natural fathers—are called, it is a reminder that a priest need not shelve either his paternal desires or his masculine human nature in order to embrace his vocation fully.

The paternal identity of the priest is an important reminder both to him and to his people: as he is to consider himself a father, they are to consider him a father as well. In its treatment of the Fourth Commandment, the *Catechism of the Council of Trent* compares the obedience of natural sons and daughters to the esteem that the Christian faithful owe to their pastors.[13] The sincere love of the Christian people will prompt them to assist their spiritual fathers with their efforts and prayers and to follow "with filial love," in the words of the Second Vatican Council, their priests "as their fathers and pastors. They should also share their priests' anxieties and help them as far as possible by prayer and active work so that they may be better able to overcome difficulties and carry out their duties with greater success."[14]

A robust narrative of celibate priestly fatherhood thereby provides clarity at a time when many, both priests and

---

[13] See *Catechism of the Council of Trent*, trans. John A. McHugh and Charles Callan (Fort Collins, CO: Roman Catholic Books, 2002), 411–415.

[14] Vatican II Council, *Presbyterorum Ordinis*, § 9.

laity, are struggling to appreciate and understand both celibacy and the priestly vocation. It is a conscious reminder that the priesthood is not simply a succession of tasks but an identity. It tells a man both what he does and who he is. It strengthens and confirms him as a father so that, with greater confidence, he can pass along the Christian identity to his people as well. In this respect alone, the re-reading of celibacy in light of paternity has the capacity to contribute decisively to renewal in the priesthood today.

WITNESS OF CELIBACY

Notwithstanding these spiritual goods derived from priestly celibacy, forgoing marriage is still seen by many as a denial of human nature, an anthropological contradiction. Celibacy is said to oppose natural sexual desires, to oppose the goods and joys of marriage and children, and therefore to oppose human maturity and growth. Even those who support and admire apostolic celibacy may quietly fear that it depreciates full human development. They may see its very sacrifice of marriage and children as proof that it is simply a gift of grace, without claim or pretension to human flourishing.

The purpose of this book has been, on the contrary, to situate celibacy within the context of human happiness and priestly maturity by demonstrating its capacity for human fulfillment and its relationship to supernatural fatherhood. In addition to these personal and ministerial benefits of celibacy, however, there are also important benefits of a wider cultural scope.

Celibacy, well lived, is a witness to human truths that are sorely needed today: incomparable lessons about the nature of parenthood, human love, and marriage.[15] These lessons also anticipate some of the human and cultural fallout should the general requirement for priestly celibacy be modified.

Universal Call to Supernatural Paternity

The first anthropological witness of celibacy was already examined in the first chapter. There are three degrees of fatherhood—biological, natural, and supernatural—and celibacy forgoes the first two in order to concentrate on the third and highest degree of paternity. It is therefore an important reminder to priest and layman alike that man's highest generative calling is in the order of grace. The celibate priest is a living witness that the most significant vocation of every biological and natural father (and mother) is exercised supernaturally when they foster their children's holiness and salvation. Indeed, every Christian is to generate supernatural life in others through his prayer, sacrifice, works of mercy, teaching, and protection of others, particularly the most vulnerable. Even if he is not a biological father, every Christian man is nonetheless called to live out the fatherhood of grace. The celibate priest, through his very celibacy and his supernatural paternity, is a witness to that important fact.

Beauty of Human Love

A second witness of celibacy is, perhaps paradoxically, a lesson about human love so needed in this sexually confused age that—however muddled—still yearns for genuine love.

---

[15] See Carter Griffin, "The Anthropological Witness of Celibacy," *Scripta Theologica* 50, no. 1 (April 2018).

One of the greatest calamities of the so-called "sexual revolution" has been an approach to love that attempts to answer that yearning in superficial and harmful ways. In the minds of many, "love" has been reduced to a sentiment that is most intensely realized in sexual expression. The nobility and goodness of the body and sexual love have, as a consequence, been devalued by the very movement that promised to overcome the perceived moralistic excesses of the past. The sexual revolution narrows the world because it strips sex of its transcendent content. Pope Benedict XVI observed that "*Eros*, reduced to pure 'sex', has become a commodity, a mere 'thing' to be bought and sold, or rather, man himself becomes a commodity. This is hardly man's great 'yes' to the body."[16]

It would be difficult to exaggerate the repercussions of the sexual revolution. Its impact on marriages with permissive divorce laws and the prevalence of contraception, on the unborn with the social and legal acceptance of abortion, on children who live with the consequences of single parenthood and broken families, on those victimized by the spread of internet pornography, and on young people who are implicitly (and often explicitly) encouraged to experiment sexually before—or without the intention of—marriage have all taken a toll on our social fabric and have damaged countless lives and families.[17] Indeed, the most vulnerable members of society—unborn babies, children, and adolescents—suffer disproportionately the effects of the sexual revolution. "This resolute refusal to recognize that the

---

[16] Pope Benedict XVI, Encyclical Letter on Christian Love *Deus Caritas Est* (December 25, 2005), § 5.

[17] See Mary Eberstadt, *Adam and Eve After the Pill: Paradoxes of the Sexual Revolution* (San Francisco: Ignatius Press, 2013).

revolution falls heaviest on the youngest and most vulnerable shoulders—beginning with the fetus and proceeding up through children and adolescents—is perhaps the most vivid example of the denial surrounding the fallout of the sexual revolution," writes scholar and author Mary Eberstadt. "In no other realm of human life," she continues, "do ordinary Americans seem so indifferent to the particular suffering of the smallest and weakest."[18]

Some years ago, Professor Allan Bloom, surveying the immediate wake of this social transformation, contended that there "are some who are men and women at the age of sixteen, who have nothing more to learn about the erotic. They are adult in the sense that they will no longer change very much. They may become competent specialists, but they are flat-souled. The world is for them what it presents itself to the senses to be; it is unadorned by imagination and devoid of ideals. This flat soul is what the sexual wisdom of our time conspires to make universal."[19] Ironically, it is love itself, he argues, that is the last victim of this misdirected search for love. "Perhaps young people do not say 'I love you,'" he writes, "because they are honest. They do not experience love—too familiar with sex to confuse it with love, too preoccupied with their own fates to be victimized by love's mad self-forgetting, the last of the genuine fanaticisms."[20]

Since celibacy is the relinquishing of marriage and physical sexual expression, it might be thought to have little to say in a discussion about human love. Undeniably, celibacy

[18] Eberstadt, *Adam and Eve After the Pill*, 29.
[19] Alan Bloom, *The Closing of the American Mind* (New York: Simon and Schuster, 1987), 134.
[20] Bloom, *The Closing of the American Mind*, 122.

has been defended at times in a way that depreciates human sexuality. Nevertheless, the tradition has never entirely lost sight of the fundamental reason for celibacy given by Christ, that it is embraced "for the sake of the kingdom of heaven" (Matt 19:12). Celibacy in this light is a positive choice of love, indeed a way of living sexual maturity, and it offers a profoundly important counterbalance to the false wisdom of the sexual revolution.

Archbishop Vigneron writes that "celibacy can be a form of sexual fulfillment, because in celibacy we can give ourselves generously, fully, sacrificially to another in a way that is certainly life-generating."[21] Indeed the notion that celibacy is emotionally or psychologically inhibiting simply defies the "testimony offered by the great majority of priests, who live their celibacy with internal freedom, rich evangelical motivation, spiritual depth, and in a panorama of strong and joyful fidelity to their vocation and mission."[22]

As observed earlier, celibacy for the Kingdom is anything but contented bachelorhood. It is, in fact, a reminder that true love is found not primarily in sexual activity but in the life of charity, which unites us to God and to one another and which alone satisfies the deep yearning for love and meaning that the sexual revolution promised, and failed, to deliver. St. Paul VI writes that "the free choice of sacred celibacy has always been considered by the Church 'as a symbol of, and stimulus to, charity': it signifies a love without reservations; it stimulates to a charity which is open to all."[23] Pope

---

[21] Allen H. Vigneron, "Can Celibacy Be Defended?," *Crisis* 18, no. 11 (December 2000): 43.

[22] Vigneron, "Can Celibacy Be Defended?" 43.

[23] Pope Paul VI, *Sacerdotalis Caelibatus*, § 24.

Francis writes that "virginity encourages married couples to live their own conjugal love against the backdrop of Christ's definitive love, journeying together toward the fullness of the Kingdom."[24]

Thus a "priest who lives a contented, enthusiastic celibate life challenges some strong cultural prejudices without so much as raising his voice," writes George Aschenbrenner.[25] His celibacy "announces that the paramount value in human life of a profoundly satisfying joy does not chiefly result from mature genital sexual activity, but from the self-gift of any loving sacrifice. These faith statements about the meaning of human life fly directly in the face of our culture's sexually fixated self-indulgence."[26] As writer Patricia Snow remarks, we "live in a world where Freudian ideas still hold sway, including the idea that religion is a sublimation of sex. The celibate, by his example, proposes a truth exactly opposite: that every other love, every lesser love, is a sublimated form of the love of God."[27] Well lived, celibacy is a compelling witness to the true nature of human love for those whom philosophical and theological arguments and even pastoral exhortations may leave unmoved.

Indeed, it is only in this context of charity that genuine sexual fulfillment can be found. Celibacy shows men and women, regardless of their vocation, that the sexual drive can and must be directed to true human flourishing. It re-

---

[24] Pope Francis, Post-Synodal Apostolic Exhortation on Love in the Family *Amoris Laetitia* (March 19, 2016), § 161.

[25] Aschenbrenner, *Quickening the Fire in Our Midst* (Chicago: Loyola Press, 2002), 125–126.

[26] Aschenbrenner, *Quickening the Fire in Our Midst*, 125–126.

[27] Patricia Snow, "Dismantling the Cross," *First Things* 252 (April 2015): 41.

veals to the world how to release love from the shackles of sexual idolatry and points the way to a life that corrects the exaggerations of the sexual revolution and gradually heals its wounds.

Celibacy is not a neutering of those who embrace it for the sake of the Kingdom; rather it is a channeling of their sexual energies toward higher goods. In the case of the celibate person, as in all people, this requires a certain discipline of life, choices to protect the gift of sexual intimacy, and an interior life to open up the currents of grace, which alone make the Christian virtue of chastity possible and beautiful. As St. John Paul II observes, "In virginity and celibacy, chastity retains its original meaning, that is, of human sexuality lived as a genuine sign of and precious service to the love of communion and gift of self to others."[28]

The Church offers perennial wisdom to those who have embraced celibacy for the Kingdom in order to safeguard the gift they have made. This same advice, and the same natural and supernatural practices outlined in the last chapter, can and should be utilized by every Christian, both married and unmarried, aspiring to live chastity well. The practices have demonstrated in countless lives that regular encounters with grace make the life of chastity possible and joyful— one of the most important lessons taught by celibacy when it is lived well.

In contrast, it is the reckless folly of our times that denies the need for grace and the steady application of self-disci-

---

[28] Pope John Paul II, Post-Synodal Apostolic Exhortation on the Formation of Priest in the Circumstances of the Present Day *Pastores Dabo Vobis* (March 15, 1992), § 29.

pline in order to experience the freedom of chastity. Shakespeare wrote in *The Tempest* that "the strongest oaths are but straw to the fire in the blood" because he understood what, in our naiveté, is overlooked today, that all our indulgence of sex and our stretching of sexual boundaries have not changed the simple power of the sexual urge and its capacity either to unite or to destroy. "An intoxicated and undisciplined *eros*," Pope Benedict XVI wrote, "is not an ascent into 'ecstasy' toward the Divine, but a fall, a degradation of man. Evidently, *eros* needs to be disciplined and purified if it is to provide not just fleeting pleasure, but a certain foretaste of the pinnacle of our existence, of that beatitude for which our whole being yearns."[29]

In addition to this witness of chastity and the means to safeguard it, by forgoing all physical sexual expression, celibates offer other irreplaceable lessons to the men and women of our time. To those who are unmarried, including those who for a variety of reasons will never marry—reasons which seem to be ever more common today—celibate men and women show that an unmarried life can nevertheless be meaningful, joyful, and healthy.

Even for those who are married there will be seasons when it is advisable or even necessary to abstain from sexual activity. Married couples may prayerfully discern that they are to abstain periodically in Natural Family Planning with the goal of spacing out births. Or couples may be physically separated for a time by professional demands or the exigencies of war. Some couples may decide, as St. Paul taught, to refrain from sexual activity for a period to

---

[29] Pope Benedict XVI, *Deus Caritas Est*, § 4.

devote themselves more fully to prayer (1 Cor 7:5). It is lived celibacy that most powerfully demonstrates the wisdom and the feasibility of living the demands of chastity in these and similar circumstances.

Celibacy, then, reveals to a world weary of failed sexual experimentation that there is a truer, nobler, and healthier road to radical love and sexual fulfillment. Those who embrace celibacy for sake of the Kingdom remind their contemporaries that all love, including sexual love, realizes its potential only when it finds its terminus in divine love and finds its protection only when guarded by virtue.

The path to chastity is admittedly hard at times, but it is the only path to genuine joy. As Pope Benedict XVI once observed to priests, "May Christianity give us joy, just as love gives joy. But love is always also a renunciation of self. The Lord himself has given us the formula of what love is: those who lose themselves find themselves; those who spare or save themselves are lost . . . joy grows and continues to mature in suffering, in communion with the cross of Christ. It is here alone that the true joy of faith is born."[30]

Dignity of Marriage

The third anthropological witness of celibacy completes the sequence of paradoxes. In the first, celibacy is thought to be a renunciation of fatherhood; yet celibacy affirms the very highest degree of fatherhood to which all men are called. In the second, celibacy is thought to be a life without human love; yet it is among the most powerful witnesses to the

[30] Pope Benedict XVI, "Address of His Holiness Benedict XVI to Diocesan Clergy of Aosta," July 25, 2005.

beauty of human love in the devastating wake of the sexual revolution. Now the third paradoxical witness: celibacy is thought to be a rejection of marriage; yet it is perhaps the brightest witness to the dignity and beauty of marriage in an age that has lost sight of both.

Celibacy, after all, only makes sense in the context of a community. Precisely because not everyone can be celibate, even from a purely natural perspective, the celibate vocation presumes a prior community of which he is a member, a community that is sustained and grows through marriage and the family. Since, moreover, apostolic celibacy is "for the sake of the kingdom," it is ordered to an augmentation of that Kingdom by fostering communion, orienting the celibate person toward the service of others. Thus St. John Paul II taught that priestly celibacy "is not only an eschatological sign; it also has a great social meaning, in the present life, for the service of the People of God. Through his celibacy, the priest becomes the 'man for others,' in a different way from the man who, by binding himself in conjugal union with a woman, also becomes, as husband and father, a man 'for others,' especially in the radius of his own family."[31]

The beginning of the Book of Genesis affirms that man is made for communion, to be in relationship (Gen 2:18). The celibate is a reminder that all people, regardless of marital status, are called to deep and meaningful relationships and to full membership in the human and ecclesial family.

More precisely, however, by sacrificing the goods of

---

[31] Pope John Paul II, "Letter of the Holy Father Pope John Paul II to All the Priests of the Church on the Occasion of Holy Thursday 1979," in *Letters to My Brother Priests* (Woodridge, IL: Midwest Theological Forum, 2006), 8.

marriage so highly esteemed by the Church, the celibate priest implicitly reveals their beauty and dignity. The "sacrifice of the human love experienced by most men in family life and given up by the priest for the love of Christ," St. Paul VI wrote, "is really a singular tribute paid to that great love. For it is universally recognized that man has always offered to God that which is worthy of both the giver and the receiver."[32] St. John Paul II stated it this way: "Virginity or celibacy for the sake of the Kingdom of God not only does not contradict the dignity of marriage but presupposes it and confirms it. Marriage and virginity or celibacy are two ways of expressing and living the one mystery of the covenant of God with His people. When marriage is not esteemed, neither can consecrated virginity or celibacy exist; when human sexuality is not regarded as a great value given by the Creator, the renunciation of it for the sake of the Kingdom of Heaven loses its meaning."[33] Raniero Cantalamessa makes the point even more strongly. He observes that celibacy has "no meaning apart from the simultaneous affirmation of marriage. If marriage were something negative, renouncing it would not be a free choice but a duty."[34]

In the Scriptures St. Paul goes so far as to say that Christ's celibacy sets the standard by which all love is measured: "Husbands, love your wives, as Christ loved the Church and gave himself up for her" (Eph 5:25). Thus, far

---

[32] Pope Paul VI, *Sacerdotalis Caelibatus*, § 50.

[33] Pope John Paul II, Apostolic Exhortation on the Role of the Christian Family in the Modern World *Familiaris Consortio* (November 22, 1981), § 16.

[34] Cantalamessa, "Dimensions of Priestly Celibacy," in *The Charism of Priestly Celibacy: Biblical, Theological, and Pastoral Reflections*, ed. John C. Cavadini (Notre Dame, IL: Ave Maria Press, 2012), 8.

from diminishing the Church's reverence for the marital vocation, St. John Paul II remarked, by "virtue of this witness, virginity or celibacy keeps alive in the Church a consciousness of the mystery of marriage and defends it from any reduction and impoverishment."[35]

At the same time, celibacy offers an important correction to an appraisal of marriage that sets it in false competition with higher goods. French poet Paul Claudel insightfully observed that "God promises by his creatures but only fulfills by himself."[36] The great good of marriage finds its highest expression not in arrogating to itself honor due to God alone but in drawing the couple ever closer to the heavenly archetype of divine love. Celibacy reminds married people "that marriage is holy, beautiful, and redeemed by Christ. It is the image of the betrothal of Christ to the Church," Cantalamessa writes, "but . . . it is not everything. It is a reality that is linked to this world and therefore transitory. It no longer exists where death no longer exists. When, as Jesus said, it will no longer be possible to die, there will be no more need to marry."[37]

Far from diminishing conjugal life, this wise corrective to exaggerated views of marriage frees it from unhealthy and unrealistic expectations. By reminding married people of the primacy of divine love, it reminds them as well

---

[35] Pope John Paul II, *Familiaris Consortio*, § 16. See, for instance, Michael Heintz, "Configured to Christ: Celibacy and Human Formation," in *The Charism of Priestly Celibacy: Biblical, Theological, and Pastoral Reflections*, ed. John C. Cavadini (Notre Dame, IL: Ave Maria Press, 2012), 74.

[36] Quoted in Snow, "Dismantling the Cross," 38.

[37] Raniero Cantalamessa, *Virginity: A Positive Approach to Celibacy for the Sake of the Kingdom of Heaven*, trans. Charles Serignat (New York: Alba House, 1995), 7–8.

that "God has made us for Himself and that therefore our hearts will always be 'unsatisfied,' until they rest in him. It is a reminder, too, that marriage and the family cannot be turned into an idol to which everything and everyone is sacrificed, a kind of absolute in life," Cantalamessa continues. "And since the first casualty of such undue absolutization is marriage itself, which is crushed by these disproportionate expectations which it will never be able to satisfy, this is why I say that virginity comes to the aid of married people themselves. It liberates marriage and each of the partners from the unbearable weight of having to be 'everything' for the other, of taking the place of God."[38]

Forgetting its relative value—that it is a means and not an end, that it is a vocation and not a right—has led to much of the current confusion regarding marriage. On the one hand, marriage seems to be considered the highest good of life and one impossible to justly withhold from anyone, including those whose relationship renders it impossible to unite in marriage due to prior marital bonds, circumstances of life, physical or mental capacity, and now even the very sexes of the couple.[39] On the other hand, this fixation on marriage is contradicted by a comparatively low estimation of the permanence of marriage, of its essential ordering to the generation of children, and of its foundational importance for social cohesion and cultural formation. The Christian who embraces celibacy for the Kingdom offers clarity in the midst of confusion through a living testimony to both the dignity and beauty of marriage as well, as its relative

---

[38] Cantalamessa, *Virginity*, 8.
[39] See Snow, "Dismantling the Cross," 40.

value compared to higher goods.

In addition to affirming the dignity of marriage and its ordering to higher goods, celibacy is a vital support to those who have embraced the marital state, in several ways.

Firstly, it is an encouragement to the life of chastity, noted above, which married couples must live in a way suited to their vocation and which is as essential in protecting their mutual love as it is in protecting the hearts of the unmarried. In their perseverance and fidelity, those who embrace celibacy offer a lived encouragement to married couples to persevere in their own demanding vocation. St. John Paul II taught that Christian couples "have the right to expect from celibate persons a good example and a witness of fidelity to their vocation until death. Just as fidelity at times becomes difficult for married people and requires sacrifice, mortification, and self-denial, the same can happen to celibate persons, and their fidelity, even in the trials that may occur, should strengthen the fidelity of married couples."[40]

Secondly, since celibate love does not engage in physical sexual expression, it depends upon other ways to show love in friendship and affection that befit different degrees and kinds of relationships. Celibacy can thus be a reminder to married couples that theirs is the highest of human friendships and that they, too, can and should express their love in a wide variety of ways, resisting a kind of affective "sloth" that gradually reduces expressions of love to physical intimacy alone. This "spectrum" of intimacy is especially important for couples that choose to engage in Natural Family Planning, since this method of fertility awareness can

---

[40] Pope John Paul II, *Familiaris Consortio*, § 16.

demand difficult periods of abstinence, often precisely when sexual desire is most intense.

Thirdly, the nature of priestly celibacy is such that, far from distancing a priest from the struggles of married persons, it confers on him a greater capacity to understand and help those in the conjugal state, as mentioned earlier. Though of course we priests have not personally experienced marriage and marital problems, we do have personal familiarity with the vocation through those we love, our parents and grandparents, our siblings, and our friends. Much of our pastoral ministry is to married couples, of all ages and walks of life, as we serve them in the joys and trials of their vocation.

More importantly, though, we have first-hand knowledge of the "vocation to love" itself—and it is precisely this wisdom that married couples and those preparing for marriage need most. Indeed, Galot cautions, if the priest were himself married, "he would also run the risk of becoming excessively engrossed in the problems of his own family. He would not be able to be open enough to the various problems of other couples."[41] Thus the "affective and mental freedom stemming from celibacy enables the priest to sympathize in greater depth with all human situations and to bring to people the help which God offers."[42]

Far from diminishing the dignity of marriage, then, or setting itself in competition with it, celibacy is perhaps the most important witness in the world today to the conjugal life. Celibacy, through its very sacrifice, both highlights the

---

[41] Galot, *Theology of the Priesthood*, trans. Roger Balducelli (San Francisco: Ignatius Press, 1984), 245–246.

[42] Galot, *Theology of the Priesthood*, 245–246.

nobility of marriage and protects it from disproportionate expectations that weigh it down and overwhelm it.

Beyond upholding the dignity of married life, celibacy points the way to marital happiness and reinforces and encourages those who have embraced the vocation. Pope Benedict XVI alluded to these lessons of celibacy at the conclusion of the Year for Priests in 2010. He pointed out that celibacy has nothing to do with simply "avoiding marriage," which can be "based on a will to live only for oneself, of not accepting any definitive tie, to have the life of every moment in full autonomy, to decide at any time what to do, what to take from life; and therefore a 'no' to the bond, a 'no' to definitiveness, to have life for oneself alone." Celibacy, he insisted, "is the opposite of this 'no', of this autonomy that accepts no obligations, which will not enter into a bond. It is the definitive 'yes' that supposes, confirms the definitive 'yes' of marriage."[43] It has been stated, in an expression highly paradoxical to many today, that "Catholic celibacy is the backbone of Catholic marriage." These important lessons taught by celibacy provide some justification for that paradox.

In light of all these anthropological witnesses of celibacy, what might the well-informed "man on the street" learn from the celibate witness of a priest?

He would learn a great deal about matters that are as provocative, as vital to his well-being, and as poorly understood as any today. He would learn from celibacy that every person is called to give life, whether biologically or not, and since the highest form of life is supernatural, it is the glory

---

[43] Pope Benedict XVI, "Dialogue of the Holy Father Benedict XVI with Priests, Conclusion of the Year for Priests," June 10, 2010.

and joy of every man to be called to be an instrument of life-giving grace to those around him, that is, to be a father in the supernatural order. He would learn from celibacy the possibility of radical love, the virtuous means to obtain and preserve it, and the joy that flows from it. In an age confused about marriage, he would learn from celibacy, through its very sacrifice of marriage, of its nobility and be reminded that marriage, if it is to be happy and fulfilling, cannot claim to satisfy a depth of yearning which only God can answer.

Truly these three lessons are more urgently needed today than ever before, in the midst of great anthropological confusion and division. They are lessons powerfully taught by the practice of celibacy—particularly among parish priests, through whom most Catholics encounter it—because they are lessons uniquely, most visibly, and most beautifully taught by those who have embraced celibacy "for the sake of the kingdom of heaven."

Saint Joseph and the Blessed Virgin Mary

SEBASTIANO DEL PIOMBO, in *The Raising of Lazarus* mentioned in the introduction, hinted at the power of Christ's generative love, his power to give life—that is, his fatherhood. Every priest is called to exercise Christ's own ministry of nourishing, healing, teaching, loving, and redeeming. He is called to be a father in the order of grace and to engender in others the seeds of supernatural life that will—please God!—blossom in eternity.

Every priest is privileged to share in this ministry, and the celibate priest is invited to do so in a unique way. It is a positive and compelling vision of celibacy, one that challenges skeptical perspectives which dismiss celibacy as a regrettable relic of the past, stunting the human maturity of the priest and perhaps even causing dangerous sexual aberrations.

When celibacy is understood to enhance the priest's very identity as a spiritual father, as coloring every fiber of his being and his priestly ministry, then it becomes a

rich source of human satisfaction, personal joy, and priestly fruitfulness. Celibacy is no longer viewed as a burden to
carry but as a gift to treasure and protect. It is the bearer
of tremendous spiritual and human gifts to the Church and
to the world at large, which would be lost or diminished
should the practice of celibacy be weakened. As St. Paul VI
wrote during the first shock waves of the sexual revolution,
"Priestly celibacy has been guarded by the Church for centuries as a brilliant jewel, and retains its value undiminished
even in our time when the outlook of men and the state of
the world have undergone such profound changes."[1]

Perhaps the greatest champions of celibacy, however, are
two individuals who themselves modeled virginal parenthood in their generative love of Jesus the High Priest: St.
Joseph and the Blessed Mother. We will conclude by turning
to their example and entrusting all of us celibate priests to
their intercession.

In the Pattern of Saint Joseph

In many respects the celibate, supernatural fatherhood of
priests finds a model in the paternity of St. Joseph. The Holy
Patriarch uniquely reflected the paternity of God as the
guardian of God's Son. St. John Paul II remarked on this singular "covenant of paternity" between Joseph and the Father,
both of whom were addressed by Jesus as "Abba."[2] Joseph
knew that "his poor house in Nazareth was filled with the

[1] Pope Paul VI, Encyclical Letter on the Celibacy of the Priest *Sacerdotalis Caelibatus* (June 24, 1967), § 1.
[2] Pope John Paul II, "Visita Pastorale nel Fucino e ad Avezzano, Omelia del Santo Padre Giovanni Paolo II. Santa Messa sul Sagrado della Cattedrale di Avezzano," March 24, 1985, author's translation.

inscrutable mystery of divine paternity, of which he himself, Joseph, was made the closest trustee and faithful servant."[3] Thus in his human nature, Christ was exposed to Joseph's professional work, his language and accent, his habits, his masculine psychology, his strength and his courage, and, above all, his human paternal affection. Joseph anticipates the spousal dimension of supernatural paternity in his marriage to Mary, who so clearly manifests and foreshadows the motherhood of the Church.

According to Pope John Paul II, St. Joseph's paternity, inserted as it is in the mystery of the Incarnation, is not simply "an 'apparent' or merely 'substitute' fatherhood. Rather, it is one that fully shares in authentic human fatherhood and the mission of a father in the family."[4] Indeed, since the fruit of his fatherhood is not an adopted or natural child, nor even a child in the order of grace, but the very source of grace and life himself, one could argue that Joseph's is the greatest instance of human fatherhood in history.

St. Joseph's supernatural paternity was therefore enhanced, not diminished, by forfeiting natural children. His fatherhood witnesses to the supernatural paternity that is to be exercised by all Christian men, specifically the fatherhood of those who embrace celibacy for the sake of the Kingdom, whether or not they are ordained priests. Joseph's paternity is a reminder that the highest form of human fatherhood is supernatural and that dedicating oneself to that

---

[3] Pope John Paul II, "Santa Messa sul Sagrado della Cattedrale di Avezzano," author's translation.

[4] Pope John Paul II, Apostolic Exhortation on the Person and Mission of Saint Joseph in the Life of Christ and of the Church Redemptoris Custos (August 15, 1989), § 21.

dimension of paternity is not limited to those with a priestly vocation, since even Joseph was not a priest.

Joseph's paternity also underscores that apostolic celibacy is not simply a question of greater physical or emotional availability, important as that consideration may be, but possesses an inner logic of its own that is ordered to supernatural fruitfulness, an openness and capacity to give oneself entirely to the good of souls in the order of grace. As Pope Benedict XVI observed during his visit to Cameroon in 2009, all fatherhood shares in the one paternity of God and "Saint Joseph is a striking case of this, since he is a father, without fatherhood according to the flesh. He is not the biological father of Jesus, whose Father is God alone, and yet he lives his fatherhood fully and completely. To be a father means above all to be at the service of life and growth."[5]

The man who embraces celibacy for the sake of supernatural generation finds in St. Joseph's "chaste love of Mary and fatherly care of Jesus" an example of engaging "all his masculine affectivity in serving Christ and the Church," writes Frederick Miller.[6] The deeply affectionate and paternal love that Joseph unquestionably had for Jesus is a reminder to celibate fathers that theirs is to be a heart overflowing with love, one writer notes, "a truly fatherly heart" that is "enriched with the tenderest sentiments of a father for his son."[7]

The humility and self-effacement that Joseph exhibited

5 Pope Benedict XVI, "Address of the Holy Father Benedict XVI at Vespers Celebration, Yaoundé, Cameroon," March 25, 2009.
6 Frederick L. Miller, "St. Joseph: Model of Celibate Love," *Homiletic and Pastoral Review* 106, no. 2 (November 2005): 23.
7 Boniface Llamera, *Saint Joseph*, trans. Sister Mary Elizabeth, OP (St. Louis, MO: B. Herder Book Co., 1962), 88.

in revealing the face of God stimulates all those who share in God's paternity, especially those who forgo marriage for the sake of supernatural fatherhood, by reminding men that their paternal authority is derived from his and is ordered above all to charity and to service.

Furthermore, St. Joseph is an apt model for the paternity specifically embraced by celibate priests. It is true that Joseph was not configured to Christ as a priest is, though one theologian does situate Joseph in a "priestly" role in the home of Nazareth as he ministered to Mary, the new Ark of the Covenant.[8] He exercised a different and in some ways unique paternity. St. John Paul II, however, nevertheless saw a personal guide for his own celibate priesthood in Joseph, whose

> life with Jesus was a continuous discovery of his own vocation as a father. He became a father in an extraordinary way, without begetting his son in the flesh. Isn't this, perhaps, an example of the type of fatherhood that is proposed to us, priests and bishops, as a model? Everything I did in the course of my ministry I saw as an expression of this kind of fatherhood—baptizing, hearing confessions, celebrating the Eucharist, preaching, admonishing, encouraging. For me these things were always a way of living out that fatherhood[9]

---

[8] See Mary Healy, "Friends of the Bridegroom: The Biblical Foundations of Priestly Celibacy," in *The Charism of Priestly Celibacy: Biblical, Theological, and Pastoral Reflections*, ed. John C. Cavadini (Notre Dame, IL: Ave Maria Press, 2012), 32.

[9] Pope John Paul II, *Rise, Let Us Be On Our Way*, trans. Walter Ziemba (New York: Warner Books, 2004), 140.

In his celibacy, the priest imitates Joseph's paternity, which was "chaste and totally dedicated to Christ and His Virgin Mother."[10] Like St. Joseph, the priest is to "engender, protect, nurture, and participate in the formation of Christ's life, sanctifying grace, in the souls of his people," Miller states. "Practicing continence for the sake of the Kingdom, as did St. Joseph, he will be continually challenged throughout his life to love the faithful more purely as his brothers and sisters, and sons and daughters."[11]

In faithfully preaching the Word of God, the priest imitates Joseph, whose life was devoted to the Word that Mary bore in her womb. In his spousal relationship with the Church, the celibate priest imitates Joseph, the faithful spouse of Mary, the image of the Church. In generating children through the power of the Holy Spirit, the priest imitates Joseph, who became a father in his marriage to Mary, who herself conceived Christ by the power of the Holy Spirit. In exercising his spiritual authority despite his unworthiness, the priest imitates Joseph who, though head of the Holy Family, was the least in perfection among the three. In protecting the Church, defending the Eucharist, preserving and cherishing the deposit of faith, and standing in readiness even to give his life if necessary to defend them, the priest imitates the guardianship of St. Joseph, who assuredly would not have hesitated to lay down his life for his two most precious treasures, Jesus and Mary.

St. Joseph, though not a priest, therefore anticipated the priest's paternity in his own life as a celibate supernatural

---

[10] Pope John Paul II, *Rise, Let Us Be On Our Way*, 140.
[11] Miller, "St. Joseph: Model of Celibate Love," 26.

father. As a man and as the Universal Patron of the Church, Joseph can continue to serve as an indispensable mentor and exemplary model for the priest whose celibacy fulfills his own paternity and hence his own masculinity.

In describing the paternity of Joseph, St. Ephrem the Syrian proposes a striking image. It was thought in his day that male palm trees generated by covering the female palms with their shade, not communicating any of their physical substance but generating, as it were, by nourishing and protecting from a distance.[12] This is the image, Ephrem gives us, of Joseph's fatherhood. He overshadowed Mary, herself the image of the Church, and her divine Son with his love, pouring himself out for them, providing for them, and protecting them, and in that love experienced his own deepest paternity and his lasting, eternal joy.

In the School of Mary

This image of an "overshadowing love" suggests as well the unique and privileged relationship that each priest enjoys with the Mother of Jesus. She is the exemplar of holiness for all Christians, including priests who are first of all to be committed disciples of the Lord. Both Mary and the priest generate supernaturally through the Holy Spirit, though in neither case is the Holy Spirit called "Father" since the Spirit does not generate from his own substance. Also like Mary, the priest generates supernaturally by responding freely and personally to the vocational grace that makes him a generator in the

---

[12] Joseph F. Chorpenning, "Francis de Sales and the Emblematic Tradition: The Palm Tree as an Allegory of St. Joseph's Virtues," in *Emblemata Sacra: Rhétorique et herméneutique du discours sacré dans la littérature en images*, eds. A. Guiderdoni and R. Dekoninck (Turnhout, Belgium: Brepols, 2007), 337n23.

order of redemption. And, like Mary, the priest is invited to generate Christ, not in the flesh as did the Blessed Virgin but in the Eucharist and in the souls of his spiritual children. Just as Mary is at once Spouse of the Holy Spirit, Mother of Jesus, and Daughter of God the Father, so is the priest at once spouse of the Church, animated by the Holy Spirit, "father" of Jesus formed in souls, and son of God the Father.

Mary, the archetype of the Church, represents the Bride through whom the priest generates new children. Like a new mother who helps draw a man out of himself toward his new paternal responsibilities, Mary can help the celibate priest discover his own fatherhood. John Cihak sees this dynamic taking place at the foot of the Cross in the noble and generous heart of St. John, one of the Lord's first priests, when the Beloved Disciple received Mary and "took her to his own home" (John 19:27). When Jesus entrusted his Mother to St. John to care for her, love her, and protect her, John Cihak remarks, this "command would resonate deeply in the heart of such a man: he must look beyond his pain and accommodate himself to her, and have all that is best about being a man rise up within him in a great act of celibate *agape.*" Cihak then continues, "The choice to be attentive to her pain brings him to the threshold of entering into his spousal love and paternity as a celibate, as the Church is coming to birth."[13]

In loving Mary, St. John the priest saw in her a reflection of his own love for Jesus but also recognized her as the pre-eminent cooperator in the Lord's continuing work on earth. When John, and all the first priests of Christ, began

---

[13] Cihak, "The Blessed Virgin Mary's Role in the Celibate Priest's Spousal and Paternal Love," *Sacrum Ministerium* 15, no. 1 (2009): 157.

to grasp the paternal privileges that had been bestowed on them in the plan of salvation, there arose a natural bond with the Lord's Mother, which remains undiminished today.

The priest's relationship to Mary, then, is not simply an adornment to the priest's ministry and interior life. Her unique role in the economy of salvation includes an inseparable and active participation in the priest's generative work, whether or not he perceives it. If he does "take her to his own home," however, the priest will find in Mary a pattern of unreserved love that can enflame his own celibate love for God's people, become a stalwart ally in his battle against sin and evil, and be a powerful source of supernatural fruitfulness.

At the beginning of this book I mentioned the danger that celibate priestly paternity might remain a compelling but ultimately impractical notion. As model and cooperator in priestly fatherhood, Mary can help ensure that the bracing vision of celibacy proposed in these pages permeates a priest's entire life and ministry. With her assistance, the priest's celibate commitment can be ordered to spiritual fatherhood, his priesthood can be exercised with a generous gift of self and the joys of paternity, and challenges to his lofty vocation can be met with healthy, faithful, and holy perseverance.

In the end, embracing paternity is a choice for each of us celibate priests, as it is for every father. The choice is not whether a priest should be a father. The choice is what kind of father he will be. On his choice depends the happiness of innumerable souls, many of whom he may never meet in this life. If he remains faithful, however, they will bear him inexpressible gratitude in eternity for the generous exercise of his celibate priestly fatherhood.

—— Acknowledgments ——

AMONG THE MANY to whom I should like to express gratitude for their inspiration of this work, I begin with my parents, Charles and Josephine Griffin, who taught me virtually everything I know about fatherhood.

I also wish to thank Fr. Robert Gahl, who gave me the initial impetus for my dissertation and who directed my doctoral work with patience and wisdom, as well as Dr. Scott Hahn, who encouraged me to write this book and whose writings were so instrumental in my conversion to the Catholic faith. I am deeply grateful to the team at Emmaus Road Publishing, including Chris Erickson, Melissa Girard, and Kate Ternus, for their motivating support and skillful assistance editing the manuscript.

So many priest mentors—true priestly fathers to me—and priest friends, to whom I owe more than I can say, have been incomparable witnesses to the joys of faithful, celibate priestly fatherhood. It is their example that I had principally in mind as I wrote these pages.

Bibliography

Aquinas, Saint Thomas. *On the Truth of the Catholic Faith (Summa Contra Gentiles) Book III: Providence.* Translated by Vernon J. Bourke. New York: Hanover House, 1955.

——. *On the Truth of the Catholic Faith (Summa Contra Gentiles) Book IV: Salvation.* Translated by Charles J. O'Neil. New York: Hanover House, 1955.

——. *Summa Theologiae.* Translated by Fathers of the English Dominican Province. New York: Benziger Bros., 1948.

——. *Super Epistolam ad Ephesios Lectura.* Rome: Marietti, 1953.

——. *Super Epistolam ad Hebraeos.* Rome: Marietti, 1953.

——. *Super Evangelium S. Ioannis Lectura.* Rome: Marietti, 1972.

Aschenbrenner, George A. *Quickening the Fire in Our Midst.* Chicago: Loyola Press, 2002.

Ashley, Benedict M. *Justice in the Church: Gender and Participation.* Washington, DC: The Catholic University of America Press, 1996.

——. *Theologies of the Body: Humanist and Christian.* Braintree, MA: The Pope John Center, 1985.

Atkinson, Joseph C. "Paternity in Crisis: Biblical and Philosophical Roots of Fatherhood." *Josephinum Journal of Theology* 9, no. 1 (Winter/Spring 2002): 3–21.

Baars, Conrad W. *A Priest for All Seasons: Masculine and Celi-*

bate. Chicago: Franciscan Herald Press, 1972.

Baker, Andrew. "Ordination and Same Sex Attraction." *America* 187 (September 30, 2002): 7–9.

Balthasar, Hans Urs von. "The Meaning of Celibacy." *Communio: International Catholic Review* 3, no. 4 (Winter 1976): 318–329.

Bloom, Alan. *The Closing of the American Mind*. New York: Simon and Schuster, 1987.

Bouyer, Louis. *Woman in the Church*. Translated by Marilyn Teichert. San Francisco: Ignatius Press, 1979.

Butler, Sara. *The Catholic Priesthood and Women: A Guide to the Teaching of the Church*. Chicago: Hillenbrand Books, 2006.

Cahall, Perry J., and James Keating. "Spiritual Fatherhood." *Homiletic and Pastoral Review* 110, no. 2 (November 2009): 14–23.

Cantalamessa, Raniero. "Dimensions of Priestly Celibacy." In *The Charism of Priestly Celibacy: Biblical, Theological, and Pastoral Reflections*, edited by John C. Cavadini, 5–26. Notre Dame, IL: Ave Maria Press, 2012.

———. *Virginity: A Positive Approach to Celibacy for the Sake of the Kingdom of Heaven*. Translated by Charles Serignat. New York: Alba House, 1995.

Catechism of the Council of Trent. Translated by John A. McHugh and Charles Callan. Fort Collins, CO: Roman Catholic Books, 2002.

Cere, Daniel. "Newman's 'Lesson of the Marriage Ring': Celibacy and Marriage in the Thought of John Henry Newman." *Louvain Studies* 22, no. 1 (1997): 59–84.

Chaput, Charles J. "The Men He Intended: Claiming Our Vocations as Priests of Jesus Christ." Accessed October 5, 2018. https://www.catholicculture.org/culture/library/view.cfm?id=7763.

Chorpenning, Joseph F. "Francis de Sales and the Emblematic Tradition: The Palm Tree as an Allegory of St. Joseph's Virtues," in *Emblemata Sacra: Rhétorique et herméneutique du discours sacré dans la littérature en images*, edited by A. Guiderdoni and R. Dekoninck, 333–347. Turnhout, Belgium: Brepols, 2007.

Cihak, John. "The Blessed Virgin Mary's Role in the Celibate Priest's Spousal and Paternal Love." *Sacrum Ministerium* 15, no. 1 (2009): 149–164.

Coakley, Paul S. "The Priest as Father 101." In *Spiritual Fatherhood: Living Christ's Own Revelation of the Father. Third Annual Symposium on the Spirituality and Identity of the Diocesan Priest, March 13–16, 2003*, edited by Edward G. Matthews. Emmitsburg, MD: Mount St. Mary's Seminary, 2003.

Cochini, Christian. *The Apostolic Origins of Priestly Celibacy*. San Francisco: Ignatius Press, 1990.

Collins, Julie A. "Celibate Love as Contemplation." *Review for Religious* 59, no. 1 (January/February 2000): 79–86.

Congregation for Bishops. *Directory for the Pastoral Ministry of Bishops* Apostolorum Successores. Vatican City State: Libreria Editrice Vaticana, 2004.

Congregation for Catholic Education. "Formation in Celibacy." *Origins* 4, no. 5 (June 27, 1974): 66–76.

Congregation for the Clergy. *Directory for the Life and Ministry of Priests*. Citta del Vaticano: Libreria Editrice Vaticana, 2013.

———. *Instruction Concerning the Criteria for the Discernment of Vocations with Regard to Persons with Homosexual Tendencies in View of their Admission to the Seminary and to Holy Orders*. London: Catholic Truth Society, 2005.

———. *The Gift of the Priestly Vocation:* Ratio Fundamentalis Institutionis Sacerdotalis. Vatican City: December 8, 2016.

Cozzens, Andrew. "Imago Vivens Iesu Christi Sponsi Eccle-

siae: The Priest as a Living Image of Jesus Christ the
Bridegroom of the Church through the Evangelical
Counsels." Diss., Pontifical University of Saint Thom-
as Aquinas, 2008.

Cozzens, Donald B. *The Changing Face of the Priesthood: A
Reflection on the Priest's Crisis of Soul.* Collegeville, MN:
The Liturgical Press, 2000.

De Avila, Juan. "Carta 1: A Un Predicador." In *Obras Completas Del Santo Maestro Juan de Avila,* edited by Francisco Martin Hernandez, vol. 5 17–28. Madrid, Spain:
Biblioteca de Autores Cristianos, 1970.

De Gaál, Emery, ed. *Homilies at a First Mass: Joseph Ratzinger's
Gift to Priests.* Translated by David Augustine. Omaha:
IPF Publications, 2016.

De Lubac, Henri. *The Motherhood of the Church.* Translated
by Sergia Englund. San Francisco: Ignatius Press,
1982.

Dickie, Jane R., Amy K. Eshleman, Dawn M. Merasco,
Amy Shepard, Michael Vander Wilt, and Melissa
Johnson. "Parent-Child Relationships and Children's
Images of God." *Journal for the Scientific Study of Reli-
gion* 36, no. 1 (March 1997): 25–43.

Dubay, Thomas. *And You are Christ's: The Charism of Virginity
and the Celibate Life.* San Francisco: Ignatius Press,
1987.

Eberstadt, Mary. *Adam and Eve After the Pill: Paradoxes of the
Sexual Revolution.* San Francisco: Ignatius Press, 2013.

Esolen, Anthony. "Over Our Dead Bodies: Men Who Are
Willing to Lay Down Their Lives Are Truly Indispensable." *Touchstone* 19, no. 5 (June 2006): 22–26.

Felices Sánchez, Fernando Benicio. *La Paternidad Espiritual
del Sacerdote: Fundamentos Teológicos de la Fecundidad
Apostólica Presbiteral.* San Juan, Puerto Rico: San Juan
de Puerto Rico, 2006.

Fernandes, Earl. "Seminary Formation and Homosexuality: Changing Sexual Morality and the Church's Response." *The Linacre Quarterly* 78, no. 3 (August 2011): 306–329.

Ferrara, Jennifer, and Sarah Hinlicky Wilson. "Ordaining Women: Two Views." *First Things* (April 2003): 33–42.

Gadenz, Pablo. "The Priest as Spiritual Father." In *Catholic for a Reason*, edited by Scott Hahn, 209–228. Steubenville, OH: Emmaus Road, 1998.

Galot, Jean. "La Motivation Évangélique du Célibat." *Gregorianum* 53, no. 4 (1972): 731–757.

———. *Theology of the Priesthood*. Translated by Roger Balducelli. San Francisco: Ignatius Press, 1984.

———. "The Priesthood and Celibacy." *Review for Religious* 24 (1965): 930–956.

Garrigou-Lagrange, Réginald. "De Paternitate Sancti Ioseph." Angelicum 22, no. 1 (1945): 105–115.

———. "La Virginité Consacrée à Dieu: Selon Saint Thomas." *Vie Spirituelle* 10 (1924): 533–550.

———. *The Trinity and God the Creator*. Translated by Frederic C. Eckhoff. St. Louis, MO: B. Herder Book Co., 1952.

Granados, José. "Priesthood: A Sacrament of the Father." *Communio: International Catholic Review* 36, no. 2 (Summer 2009): 186–218.

Griffin, Carter. "Supernatural Fatherhood through Priestly Celibacy: Fulfillment in Masculinity (A Thomistic Study)." Diss., Pontifical University of the Holy Cross, 2011.

———. "The Anthropological Witness of Celibacy." *Scripta Theologica* 50, no. 1 (April 2018): 121–138.

Hahn, Scott. *Many Are Called: Rediscovering the Glory of the Priesthood*. New York: Doubleday, 2010.

———. "The Paternal Order of Priests." In *Spiritual Fatherhood: Living Christ's Own Revelation of the Father. Third*

Annual Symposium on the Spirituality and Identity of the Diocesan Priest, March 13–16, 2003, edited by Edward G. Matthews. Emmitsburg, MD: Mount St. Mary's Seminary, 2003.

Harrison, Verna. "Gender, Generation, and Virginity in Cappadocian Theology." *Journal of Theological Studies* 47, no. 1 (April 1996): 38–68.

Hauke, Manfred. *Women in the Priesthood? A Systematic Analysis in the Light of the Order of Creation and Redemption.* Translated by David Kipp. San Francisco: Ignatius Press, 1988.

Healy, Mary. "Friends of the Bridegroom: The Biblical Foundations of Priestly Celibacy." In *The Charism of Priestly Celibacy: Biblical, Theological, and Pastoral Reflections,* edited by John C. Cavadini, 27–46. Notre Dame, IL: Ave Maria Press, 2012.

Heid, Stefan. *Celibacy in the Early Church: The Beginnings of Obligatory Continence for Clerics in East and West.* San Francisco: Ignatius Press, 2001.

Heintz, Michael. "Configured to Christ: Celibacy and Human Formation." In *The Charism of Priestly Celibacy: Biblical, Theological, and Pastoral Reflections,* edited by John C. Cavadini, 65–84. Notre Dame, IL: Ave Maria Press, 2012.

Hennessy, Thomas E. D. *The Fatherhood of the Priest.* Somerset, OH: The Rosary Press, 1950.

——. "The Fatherhood of the Priest." The Thomist 10, no. 3 (July, 1947): 271–306.

Hildebrand, Dietrich von. *In Defense of Purity: An Analysis of the Catholic Ideals of Purity and Virginity.* London: Sheed and Ward, 1940.

Horn, Wade F. "The Rise of an American Fatherhood Movement." In *The Faith Factor in Fatherhood: Renewing the Sacred Vocation of Fathering,* edited by Don E. Eberly, 131–144. Lanham, MD: Lexington Books, 1999.

Jaki, Stanley L. "Man of One Wife or Celibacy." *Homiletic and Pastoral Review* 86, no. 4 (January 1986): 18–25.

———. *Theology of Priestly Celibacy.* Front Royal, VA: Christendom, 1997.

Kentenich, Joseph. *Rediscovering the Father: Selected Texts for the Year of God the Father.* Mumbai, India: St. Paul Press, 1999.

Lewis, C. S. *The Four Loves.* San Diego: Harcourt Brace Jovanovich, 1960.

Lienhard, Joseph T. "Origins and Practice of Priestly Celibacy in the Early Church." In *The Charism of Priestly Celibacy: Biblical, Theological, and Pastoral Reflections,* edited by John C. Cavadini, 47–64. Notre Dame, IL: Ave Maria Press, 2012.

Llamera, Boniface. *Saint Joseph.* Translated by Sister Mary Elizabeth, OP. St. Louis, MO: B. Herder Book Co., 1962.

Lock, Timothy G. "Same-Sex Attractions as a Symptom of a Broken Heart: Psychological Science Deepens Respect, Compassion, and Sensitivity." In *Living the Truth in Love: Pastoral Approaches to Same-Sex Attraction,* edited by Janet E. Smith and Paul Check, 244–278. San Francisco: Ignatius Press, 2015.

Manning, Henry Edward. *The Eternal Priesthood.* Baltimore: John Murphy and Co., 1883.

Mansini, Guy, and Lawrence J. Welch. "In Conformity to Christ." *First Things* 162 (April 2006): 13–16.

Margerie, Bertrand de. *Christ for the World: The Heart of the Lamb.* Translated by Malachy Carroll. Chicago: Franciscan Herald Press, 1973.

May, William. "The Mission of Fatherhood." *Josephinum Journal of Theology* 9, no. 1 (Winter–Spring 2002): 42–55.

McGovern, Thomas. *Priestly Celibacy Today.* Princeton, NJ: Scepter, 1998.

———. *Priestly Identity: A Study in the Theology of Priesthood.* Dublin, Ireland: Four Courts Press, 2002.

Mead, Margaret. *Male and Female.* Harmondsworth, UK: Penguin Books, 1950.

Miller, Frederick L. "St. Joseph: Model of Celibate Love." *Homiletic and Pastoral Review* 106, no. 2 (November 2005): 22–27.

———. *The Grace of Ars.* San Francisco: Ignatius Press, 2010.

Miller, John W. *Biblical Faith and Fathering: Why We Call God 'Father'.* New York: Paulist Press, 1989.

———. "The Idea of God as Father." In *The Faith Factor in Fatherhood: Renewing the Sacred Vocation of Fathering,* edited by Don E. Eberly, 203–218. Lanham, MD: Lexington Books, 1999.

Miller, Monica Migliorino. *Sexuality and Authority in the Catholic Church.* Scranton, PA: University of Scranton Press, 2006.

———. "The Gender of the Holy Trinity." *New Oxford Review* 70, no. 5 (May 2003): 27–35.

Nyathi, Jerome Rono. "Priesthood Today and the Crisis of Fatherhood: Fatherlessness in Africa with Special Reference to Zimbabwe." Diss., Pontifical University of Saint Thomas Aquinas, 2002.

O'Callaghan, Paul. "Gli Stati di Vita del Cristiano: Riflessioni su un'Opera di Hans Urs von Balthasar." *Annales Theologici* 21 (2007): 61–100.

Ong, Walter J. *Fighting for Life: Contest, Sexuality, and Consciousness.* Ithaca, NY: Cornell University Press, 1981.

Peach, Andrew. "On the Demise of Fatherhood." *First Things: On the Square* (June 17, 2009). Accessed October 5, 2018. http://www.firstthings.com/onthesquare/2009/6/on-the-demise-of-fatherhood.

Pope Benedict XVI. "Address by His Holiness Pope Benedict XVI to the Clergy, Warsaw Cathedral." May 25, 2006.

———. "Address of His Holiness Benedict XVI to Diocesan Clergy of Aosta." July 25, 2005.

———. "Address of His Holiness Benedict XVI to the Members of the Roman Curia at the Traditional Exchange of Christmas Greetings." December 22, 2006.

———. "Address of the Holy Father Benedict XVI at Vespers Celebration, Yaoundé, Cameroon." March 25, 2009.

———. "Christ is Never Absent in the Church, General Audience." April 14, 2010.

———. "Dialogue of the Holy Father Benedict XVI with Priests, Conclusion of the Year for Priests." June 10, 2010.

———. Encyclical Letter on Christian Love *Deus Caritas Est*. December 25, 2005.

———. "In Priests the Audacity of a God Close to Us: Mass in St. Peter's Square for Conclusion of the Year for Priests." June 11, 2010.

———. *Jesus of Nazareth*. New York: Doubleday, 2007.

———. *Light of the World*. San Francisco: Ignatius Press, 2010.

Pope Francis. Apostolic Exhortation on the Proclamation of the Gospel in Today's World *Evangelii Gaudium*. November 24, 2013.

———. "Morning Meditation in the Chapel of the *Domus Sanctae Marthae*: The Joy of Fatherhood." June 26, 2013.

———. Post-Synodal Apostolic Exhortation on Love in the Family *Amoris Laetitia*. March 19, 2016.

Pope John Paul II. Apostolic Exhortation on the Person and Mission of Saint Joseph in the Life of Christ and of the Church *Redemptoris Custos*. August 15, 1989.

———. Apostolic Exhortation on the Role of the Christian Family in the Modern World *Familiaris Consortio*.

November 22, 1981.

——. "A Priest is as Good as His Eucharistic Life: Pope to Italian Clergy." February 16, 1984.

——. "La Vocazione al Ministero é una Scelta d'Amore: Omelia del Santo Padre Giovanni Paolo II. Santa Messa di Inaugurazione del Convegno 'Spiritualità del Presbitero Diocesano Oggi.'" November 4, 1980.

——. "Letter of the Holy Father Pope John Paul II to All the Priests of the Church on the Occasion of Holy Thursday 1979." In *Letters to My Brother Priests*, 8–25. Woodridge, IL: Midwest Theological Forum, 2006.

——. Post-Synodal Apostolic Exhortation on the Formation of Priest in the Circumstances of the Present Day *Pastores Dabo Vobis*. March 15, 1992.

——. *Rise, Let Us Be On Our Way*. Translated by Walter Ziemba. New York: Warner Books, 2004.

——. "The Church is Committed to Priestly Celibacy, General Audience." July 17, 1993.

——. "Visita Pastorale nel Fucino e ad Avezzano, Omelia del Santo Padre Giovanni Paolo II. Santa Messa sul Sagrado della Cattedrale di Avezzano." March 24, 1985.

Pope Paul VI. Encyclical Letter on the Celibacy of the Priest *Sacerdotalis Caelibatus*. June 24, 1967.

Pope Pius XI. Encyclical Letter on the Catholic Priesthood *Ad Catholici Sacerdotii*. December 20, 1935.

Pope Pius XII. "Allocution to Married Couples." January 15, 1941.

——. Apostolic Exhortation on the Development of Holiness in Priestly Life *Menti Nostrae*. September 23, 1950.

——. "Discourse of His Holiness Pius XII to the Parish Priests of Rome and the Lenten Preachers." February 6, 1940.

——. Encyclical Letter on Consecrated Virginity *Sacra*

Virginitas. March 25, 1954.

Radcliffe, Timothy. "Can Gays Be Priests?" *The Tablet* (November 26, 2005): 4–5.

Ratzinger, Joseph. *Introduction to Christianity.* Translated by J. R. Foster. San Francisco: Ignatius Press, 1990.

———. "Some Perspectives on Priestly Formation Today (Keynote at Symposium on Priestly Formation at St. Charles Borromeo Seminary)." January 20, 1990.

Rousseau, Mary F. "Pope John Paul II's Letter on the Dignity and Vocation of Women: The Call to Communio." *Communio: International Catholic Review* 16, no. 2 (Summer 1989): 212–232.

Ryan, Peter. "Second Response to 'Self-Gift in Generative Love.'" In *Spiritual Fatherhood: Living Christ's Own Revelation of the Father. Third Annual Symposium on the Spirituality and Identity of the Diocesan Priest, March 13–16, 2003,* edited by Edward G. Matthews, Emmitsburg, MD: Mount St. Mary's Seminary, 2003.

Saint John of the Cross. "The Ascent of Mount Carmel." Book 3, chap. 45. In *The Collected Works of St. John of the Cross,* translated by Kieran Kavanaugh, OCD, and Otilio Rodriguez, OCD, 349. Washington, DC: ICS Publications, 1991.

Saraiva Martins, Jose. "Training for Priestly Celibacy." Accessed October 5, 2018. http://www.vatican.va/roman_curia/congregations/cclergy/documents/rc_con_cclergy_doc_01011993_train_en.html.

Sartain, J. Peter. "Beloved Disciples at the Table of the Lord: Celibacy and the Pastoral Ministry of the Priest." In *The Charism of Priestly Celibacy: Biblical, Theological, and Pastoral Reflections,* edited by John C. Cavadini, 125–142. Notre Dame, IL: Ave Maria Press, 2012.

Scheeben, Matthias Joseph. *The Mysteries of Christianity.*

Translated by Cyril Vollert. St. Louis, MO: B. Herder Book Co., 1946.

Selin, Gary. *Priestly Celibacy: Theological Foundations.* Washington, DC: The Catholic University of America Press, 2016.

Sheed, Frank. *Theology and Sanity.* San Francisco: Ignatius Press, 1993.

Sheen, Fulton. *The World's First Love.* 1952. Reprint, San Francisco: Ignatius Press, 2011.

Smith, Janet. *The Fatherhood of God.* Denver, CO: Unpublished Manuscript, 2000.

Snow, Patricia. "Dismantling the Cross." *First Things* 252 (April 2015): 33–42.

Stafford, J. Francis. "The Eucharistic Foundations of Sacerdotal Celibacy." *Origins* 23, no. 12 (September 2, 1993): 211–216.

Stickler, Alphonso M. *The Case for Clerical Celibacy: Its Historical Development and Theological Foundations.* San Francisco: Ignatius Press, 1995.

Sutton, Philip M. "The Fatherhood Moment: The Rest of the Story." In *Marriage and the Common Good: Proceedings from the Twenty-Second Annual Convention of the Fellowship of Catholic Scholars, September 24–26, 1999, Deerfield, Illinois,* edited by Kenneth D. Whitehead, 62–77. South Bend, IN: St. Augustine's Press, 2001.

Teresa of Calcutta. "Priestly Celibacy: A Sign of the Charity of Christ" (1993). Accessed October 5, 2018. http://www.vatican.va/roman_curia/congregations/cclergy/documents/rc_con_cclergy_doc_01011993_sign_en.html.

Touze, Laurent. "Paternidad Divina y Paternidad Sacerdotal." *XX Simposio Internacional de Teología de la Universidad de Navarra.* Pamplona, Spain: Servicio de Publicaciones de la Universidad de Navarra, 2000: 655–664.

Trochu, Francis. *The Curé d'Ars: St. Jean-Marie-Baptiste Vianney*. Westminster, MD: The Newman Press, 1949.

Vatican II Council. Decree on Priestly Training *Optatam Totius*. October 28, 1965.

———. Decree on the Ministry and Life of Priests *Presbyterorum Ordinis*. December 7, 1965.

———. Dogmatic Constitution on the Church *Lumen Gentium*. November 21, 1964.

Vigneron, Allen H. "Can Celibacy Be Defended?" *Crisis* 18, no. 11 (December 2000): 42–46.

———. "Christ's Virginal Heart and His Priestly Charity." *Chaste celibacy: living Christ's own spousal love: Sixth Annual Symposium on the Spirituality and Identity of the Diocesan Priest, March 15–18, 2007*. Omaha, NE: The Institute for Priestly Formation, 2007.

———. "The Virginity of Jesus and the Celibacy of His Priests." In *The Charism of Priestly Celibacy: Biblical, Theological, and Pastoral Reflections*, edited by John C. Cavadini, 85–108. Notre Dame, IL: Ave Maria Press, 2012.

Vitz, Paul C. "The Father Almighty, Maker of Male and Female." *Touchstone* 14, no. 1 (January–February 2001): 33–39.

———. "The Importance of Fathers: Evidence from Social Science." Accessed October 11, 2018. https://www.catholiceducation.org/en/controversy/marriage/family-decline-the-findings-of-social-science.html.

Vitz, Paul C., and Daniel C. Vitz. "Messing with the Mass: The Problem of Priestly Narcissism Today." *Homiletic and Pastoral Review* 108, no. 2 (November 2007): 16–22.

———. "Priests and the Importance of Fatherhood." *Homiletic and Pastoral Review* 109, no. 3 (December 2008): 16–22.

Ware, Kallistos. *The Spiritual Father in St. John Climacus and St. Symeon the New Theologian*. Kalamazoo, MI: Cistercian Publications, 1989.

Weinandy, Thomas Gerard. "Of Men and Angels." *Nova et Vetera* 3, no. 2 (2005): 295–306.

Wojtyla, Karol. *Love and Responsibility*. Translated by H. T. Willetts. New York: Farrar, Straus, Giroux, 1981.